fearlessly
different

fearlessly different

an autistic actor's journey to broadway's biggest stage

Mickey Rowe

ROWMAN & LITTLEFIELD
Lanham • Boulder • New York • London

Published by Rowman & Littlefield
An imprint of The Rowman & Littlefield Publishing Group, Inc.
4501 Forbes Boulevard, Suite 200, Lanham, Maryland 20706
www.rowman.com

Distributed by NATIONAL BOOK NETWORK

6 Tinworth Street, London, SE11 5AL, United Kingdom

British Library Cataloguing in Publication Information Available

Library of Congress Cataloging-in-Publication Data Available

Names: Rowe, Mickey, 1988– author.
Title: Fearlessly different : an autistic actor's journey to Broadway's biggest stage / Mickey Rowe.
Description: Lanham : Rowman & Littlefield, [2022] | Includes index. | Summary: "Fearlessly Different is the moving, inspirational memoir of autistic actor Mickey Rowe, who pushed beyond the stereotypes and obstacles so many disabled individuals face to shine on Broadway's biggest stage. Fearlessly Different opens up the world of autism to those who feel locked out and helps those with autism feel seen and understood"— Provided by publisher.
Identifiers: LCCN 2021029539 (print) | LCCN 2021029540 (ebook) | ISBN 9781538163122 (cloth) | ISBN 9781538163139 (epub)
Subjects: LCSH: Rowe, Mickey, 1988- | Actors—United States—Biography. | Autistic people—United States—Biography.
Classification: LCC PN2287.R773 A3 2022 (print) | LCC PN2287.R773 (ebook) | DDC 792.02/8092 [B]—dc23
LC record available at https://lccn.loc.gov/2021029539
LC ebook record available at https://lccn.loc.gov/2021029540

disclaimer

In this book some people's names and identifying features have been changed to respect their anonymity. I ask that you also respect everyone in this book to the very best of your ability. While the chronology of some events has been compressed to keep this book to a readable length, I have documented the events in this book to the absolute best of my memory at this time. Even still, I am sure that some of the people in this story may remember things differently or have different perspectives than my own. And that is okay. There is room for a multitude of perspectives. Our differences are our strengths.

This book is dedicated to you, holding this book, who have at times felt so different and so alone.

Though I suppose all good books are dedicated to a single person, aren't they? So rather, to the trailblazing immigrant Helen Marion, for being my best friend.

Or rather still, to myself *and* the trailblazing immigrant Helen Marion . . . before we were friends, for at that time we both felt so different and so alone. How sweet it is that we are still different, but no longer alone.

And to you, dear reader. For being my new friend. Thank you.

acknowledgments

I would like to acknowledge the many people without whose work this book would not exist: the mountain-moving Helen Marion; my incredible agent Allison Hellegers and Stimola Literary Studio; my brilliant editor Christen Karniski as well as the entire team at Rowman & Littlefield; my publicists Deb Shapiro, Elizabeth Shreve, and Suzanne Williams at Shreve Williams; and most importantly, the generations of disability rights activists who have come before me, especially Dominick Ławniczak Evans, Lydia X. Z. Brown, Lawrence Carter-Long, Alice Wong, Haben Girma, Christine DeZinno Bruno, and Sara Luterman, I am standing on all of your shoulders.

prologue

Enter this book with me and I will be your guide into a world you *might* find deeply mysterious: the world of autism. A world that you *may* feel is locked away and impossible for you to even begin to understand. As distant and mysterious as the Mariana Trench or the dark side of the moon. Perhaps this is similar to how you may think a nonspeaking autistic child, rocking and flapping their hands, might be incapable of understanding your world. Well, as an autistic and legally blind person in a society designed by and for nondisabled people, it has always been made clear to me all the things that I am apparently incapable of doing.

In this book I'll share with you the story of how I did it all anyway, because of and not in spite of my autism. Though being autistic in our culture has made my life incalculably harder, I still know that my differences are my strengths, and so are yours.

I hope that this book encourages and emboldens you—whether you are autistic or not—by showing you that the things that make you different, or that you might even perceive as your weaknesses, actually make you unique and valuable and might even be your biggest strengths. We all share this in common because in the end, the story of autism is the story of being human.

If I can have hope, we all can. If I can start a dialogue, we all can. If I can effect change, we all can.

You will join me on the swashbuckling adventures of a lone pirate adrift on the Salish Sea, to feeling a student's mouth and body left aching and frustrated after lengthy days of mainstream school, Special education, occupational therapy, and speech therapy. You will follow in the teetering, towering footsteps of a child who didn't know how to make a friend but instead learned to engage with the world as a character in the colorful, spectacular world of stilt walking and street performing. Don a helmet and crave proprioceptive input with me as we hurtle down the side of a volcano on a unicycle. I'll let you into my experiences of deepest love: from the crushing challenges and unique successes of being a young, single autistic father with full custody of his autistic child, to why nonautistics should be jealous they don't get to experience sex as an autistic person.

Before we begin, if you are nonautistic, I'm going to ask you to take a moment to relax your grip on everything you thought you knew about autism.

Ready? Okay.

Now follow me through the dark from stage right, find our mark center stage, and blink out of momentary blindness underneath the sharp and sudden brightness of a spotlight burning down on Broadway's biggest stage. This is where our story begins.

1

Life is either a daring adventure, or nothing.

—Helen Keller

I am standing alone, starkly center stage in Broadway's biggest theatre, with what feels like Broadway's brightest spotlight radiantly burning down on me. The brash beam of light tingles as it warms my skin. I feel the prickle of moisture tickling my hairline; I want to wipe it, but I don't want to look fidgety. Everyone expects me to be fidgety.

"Ok everyone, take a ten."

The stage manager's voice slices through the speakers, and the spotlight cuts off as sharply as it had first burst on.

Today was one long whirlwind of activity as all the technical elements that would come together for tonight's star-studded fundraiser were being coordinated. I am giving the keynote speech, and I am unendingly thankful that the rehearsing part of the programming is over. I am finally able to get my bearings.

I descend from the stage and begin to roam, walking alone through the house of the cavernous Gershwin Theatre, home of the Tony Award–winning *Wicked* on Broadway. There is nowhere more magical than to be in an empty theatre. My eyes scan the room, taking in the expertly crafted, velvety blue-gray seats. A deep and peaceful ocean that will soon be whipped into a maelstrom as people flood in to hear Kelli O'Hara sing, and then witness a "real-life" autistic person speaking to them delivering the keynote at this big-name charity event. There is some quietly lingering "performing monkey" sense about it all, but it's overwhelmed by a sense of awe. Who would have thought that a legally blind three-year-old who could only communicate with his own made-up sign language would end up here? As an autistic child, I was sure that no one cared about my thoughts, my perspective. And yet, today I will fill a theatre with people from all walks of life, all interested in hearing about my experiences living in a world set up by and for nonautistic people.

The awe never really goes away. I have had the privilege of spending much of the year so far doing the same thing as I will tonight, at distinguished establishments such as the Lincoln Center, the Kennedy Center, and Yale. The year has been a flurry of whirlwind speaking engagement trips. This trip, though, I feel at rest for the first time, settled in the center of the whirlwind. Earlier this morning, sitting in a New York diner eating corned beef hash and drinking coffee, I felt at home in my own skin. It was so much different than two years earlier, when I embarked on my first solo trip anywhere. I was flown out from Seattle to New York City to audition for the leading role in the only play on Broadway with an autistic lead character: Christopher Boone in *The Curious Incident of the Dog in the Night-Time*. That was my first time traveling on my own, and I felt a bit like Christopher, an overwhelmed autistic person taking my own adventure, submerged in one of the busiest cities on earth.

The city. The sensory overload. To get myself from one moment to the next I had to repeatedly remind myself: be fearless in the pursuit of your goals, be courageous in the pursuit of what you know is right. Like a mantra I had written for myself.

Curious Incident and being the first openly autistic actor to play an autistic character professionally has completely changed my life, and now here I am, in airports and hotels feeling like the proverbial fish out of water. Funnily enough, I do think to myself sometimes that I am in general a bit like a fish: I like to keep moving. Swinging, rocking. It helps me focus. My whole life I've been discouraged from visibly autistic behaviors like rocking back and forth, but over the course of my adult life, I've decided that if a meeting is dragging, a little bit of movement sure helps me lock back in. I've finessed it enough to find the balance of moving enough to focus and regulate myself but doing so where it doesn't concern or worry nonautistic people. Nonautistic people seem to be easily worried by my movements.

I study the velvety seats, one by one. Who will sit in this one? Maybe a parent of an autistic child, simply wanting some reassurance that everything will be okay. They're wanting to head home tonight feeling encouraged that their child does indeed have a shot at falling in love and having a family of their own—what they feel is leading a "normal life." They're hoping that seeing an autistic person delivering a keynote speech on a Broadway stage will give their weary hearts a rejuvenating jolt, so they can keep the faith that despite the fact that 85 percent of college graduates on the autism spectrum are unemployed, their child can actually make it into that elusive 15 percent of autistic college graduates with a job.[1] I know these parents. They flood my inbox regularly, grasping and aching for me to calm their fears of the unknown.

How about this seat? Maybe here will be a person who is incredibly skeptical about the quality of content I will deliver tonight. They expect to leave feeling proud of how noble they were to encouragingly nod and clap at a developmentally delayed person piecing together simple words about his hard times in life. Maybe they will try to wait around after to clasp my hand while slowly and clearly telling me they were so *inspired* by my speech; did I write it all by myself? Wow!! I know these people too. They are the teachers, the family friends who thought I was too dim to notice them speaking in hushed tones about delays and retardation, voices brightening when I came close, being oh so Very Encouraging of the most simple things I did.

I'm sure these types of people and more will fill these seats tonight. I finally break my gaze from the repetitive rows of chairs, looking up to see the mammoth set pieces being stored above the stage, hoisted up by giant pulleys. It looks like all available space above the stage is filled, meticulously hung with lights, speakers, and all other manner of bare-bones elements that are primed and ready to burst into life at the word of a stage manager, stunning spellbound audiences with spectacular theatre magic and special effects. There is nothing sensory friendly about the brash fullness of what they are capable of unleashing. But there is nothing sensory friendly about the world I live in either. Like many autistic people, I have sensory processing disorder. This city is a continual assault on all senses. I'm grateful to have found my ways of navigating a world that is not sensory friendly. Headphones, V-neck shirts, the subtle clenching and unclenching of a fist.

"Mr. Rowe?" Interruption. I turn to see a production assistant, hugging a clipboard and clutching a Starbucks cup. "Your dressing room is ready for you now. This way." I thank them and follow their lead. Up onto the stage, off through a wing, down a hallway, on my right. I look back the way we came, remembering this route for later. They are saying some helpful information about the room, I'm sure, but I'm busy taking it all in.

The familiar: lights around the mirrors, a rack neatly packed with elaborate costuming, wig forms evenly spaced above the rack.

The unfamiliar: the wig form is not right, an emerald bathtub ring of makeup staining the canvas head.

Then it hits me: that green crown of schmear can only mean one thing! I realize that I am in the dressing room of the misunderstood Elphaba, one of the two leading roles in *Wicked*. I look around, and more of her world pops out at me. The dark green gowns, green makeup, and the rest, waiting to be used again to turn the actress into the verdantly hued witch the next day.

I was a lonely autistic high schooler, bag full of behemoth large-print textbooks, pacing the hallways with no friends, going home after soulless special education to cover my ears with my fists in the corner of my room. *How did I get from there to being here surrounded by magic?* Just weeks before, I escaped the most confusing, cold-sweat inducing, and skin-crawling situation of my life. Fleeing danger one morning before the sun came up, my heart racing, with my autistic son in hand. But now I force myself to forget that and pretend it never happened. I tuck my thumb inside my fist. I squeeze my thumb once. Then twice.

Rehearsal may be over for me, but I know that in moments the camera crew from *HuffPost* will arrive to wire me up with microphones for an interview. They will poke and pry into my mind; then soon after it will be almost time for me to get back onstage, this time before an ocean of filled seats. Until then, this is my moment of peace, kept company by a host of green treasures.

You may ask yourself, what is an autistic "adult"—although I still think of myself as a boy most often—doing speaking in front of thousands of people as an actor? I often ask myself that question, but less and less these days, because I learned to shift my thinking and believe a statement that has profoundly changed my life: my differences are my strengths.

In what seems like the blink of an eye, the moment of peace has passed, the procedurally probing interview has come and gone, and I am back under that piercing spotlight. Although thousands of eyes are fixed on me now, an easy relief washes over me; gratefulness that these words have tumbled from my tongue enough times to be somewhat muscle memory. I can relax just enough to relish in this moment: center stage at the hallowed Gershwin Theatre. With 1933 seats, it's the largest house on Broadway, and tonight the expansive cavern seems bursting at the seams, packed with people hanging on my every word. I feel like I'm bursting at the seams too. Clench fist once, twice. Relax.

I begin my speech.

"If you see me walking down the street, I most likely have headphones on. I nearly always wear a blue T-shirt, V-neck so nothing touches my neck. I was late to speak, but I invented my own incredibly detailed sign language to communicate. I had speech therapy all through elementary school, occupational therapy all through middle school, and was in special ed for part of the day through high school. Being on the autism spectrum growing up and through high school I had no friends. I spent my lunch breaks and recesses just pacing the hallways not knowing who to talk to, how to talk to them, or how to make a friend. I was completely alone in my own head. . . ."

Such familiar phrases. My mind feels reassured and safe enough to wander again, and though I keep addressing my enraptured audience, inside my mind I remember my journey in vivid detail.

2

Courage doesn't always roar. Sometimes courage is the little voice at the end of the day that says "I'll try again tomorrow."

—Mary Anne Radmacher

America loves to speculate in hushed tones about what "causes autism." Gluten, medications, metals. Some parents are so fearful that they might end up with a kid with autism that they avoid effective vaccines for preventable diseases, as if the only thing worse than a child dying is a child with autism.

I was a preemie, born with underdeveloped eyes. Preemies *are* statistically more likely to be diagnosed with autism spectrum disorder.[1] My first experiences of the outside world were in the NICU, with my tiny body attached to a caffeine drip, which keeps preemies' minute hearts beating and minuscule lungs breathing. That caffeine drip was my lifeline. Some things never change because I still love my daily Starbucks grande latte, the caffeine fueling my dopamine receptors. It's funny how some of the things that bring me comfort now had already found me back then when I was alone in the hospital. Unfortunately, my being in the NICU didn't bring the same comfort to my mom, Sandy.

Studies have shown that 10 to 15 percent[2] of new moms experience postpartum depression. For moms with babies in the NICU, that figure leaps to as high as 70 percent.[3] The feelings of guilt and helplessness are often very overwhelming for new parents, and many report difficulties feeling bonded to their new baby. I am certain this was the case for my mother.

Many parents of autistic children also have trouble bonding with their children. In fact, people with developmental disabilities are the most likely of any group to be killed by their parents and caregivers. According to a Ruderman Family Foundation report that documented more than two hundred deaths from 2011 to 2015, at least one disabled person is killed per week by their parent or caregiver.[4] At least one per week! When a nondisabled child is killed by their parent or caregiver, society's response is one of unequivocal outrage and disgust. "Let the murderer rot in jail," they demand. "There is a special place in hell reserved for such despicable parents," they howl. And yet, if the filicide of a disabled child makes the news, the blame is assigned to the victim.

Alex Spourdalakis, for example, was fourteen when his mother and godmother decided to kill him. Alex was autistic. His mother and godmother stabbed him four times in the chest and slit his wrists. When the media talked about his death, they sympathized with his mother, stating, "Alex's mother said she did not want him in an institution, which she thought would be a form of torture, according to police. The women also killed the family cat, authorities said, because Spourdalakis didn't want authorities to take it to a shelter."[5]

People are told to feel sympathy for the murderer because no one could understand or judge how hard it must be to raise a child with a disability. We are assured that the parent was an otherwise excellent parent who just snapped under an unbearable load. Our ableist society (meaning a society that favors nondisabled people) believes that it is better to be dead than disabled. Although many would stop short of saying it bluntly, enough people are truly ignorant in their belief that the murderer did themselves, the victim, and the entire world a favor. The news and legal systems often christen the murder of an autistic child as a mercy killing.

When ABC News ran a story about fourteen-year-old Alex's death, the news report said, "The psych facilities wouldn't take him. . . . So where's the help for the parents? There's no support for them, there's no relief. No respite, nowhere for them to safely bring their children . . . Alex will not have to suffer anything, anymore. . . . She just, she just couldn't take seeing her son in pain anymore and seeing no future for him. . . . Alex will not be treated as less than human. . . . Alex will not have to suffer anything, anymore."[6]

I wonder, with one of these murders happening every week, how many more will die before the general public begins to hear about it.

In light of those statistics, it is disappointing yet unsurprising that my mother was unable to form a bond with her autistic preemie. I have never been told baby stories about myself, other than that I was left strapped in my car seat for much of the time, even while in the house. Somewhere in my early years it is likely that my parents were informed that I was autistic. They chose to never share this information with me. These silences all speak volumes.

I was nonspeaking throughout my earliest years. It is such a damaging misconception that nonspeaking autistic people don't speak because they are simply not smart enough. We live in an inherently ableist society that uses the word "dumb" interchangeably with the word "stupid." But when you take a moment to think critically about what society tells you is acceptable, you realize that just as "blind" means cannot see and "deaf" means cannot hear, "dumb" actually means cannot speak. I'm here to tell you that although I couldn't speak, I was certainly not stupid, and I still understood everything everyone else was saying. This is the case for many nonspeaking autistic people.

The medical term is "aphasia." Simply put, it means you understand what is being said to you and you know what you want to say, but you are unable to say it. Somewhere between your brain and your mouth the train goes off the rails. It's not that mysterious and it's not limited to autistic people. If anyone, autistic or not, simply sustains a concussion, they may show symptoms of aphasia. But if you put a communication application, even a keyboard, in front of a nonspeaking autistic person, chances are they may communicate more eloquent and perceptive thoughts than you. It's funny how the less we speak, and the more we observe and listen, the more we in fact have to productively contribute.

As Shakespeare says, "The more pity that fools may not speak wisely what wise men do foolishly."

The thing is, in order to make this kind of communication possible, you must take the burden off the disabled person to communicate in the way that is easiest for you, and put the burden on yourself to communicate in the way that is easiest for the person with a disability. It requires that you have a belief in their intelligence and ability and a desire to hear what they have to say, as well as a commitment to working with them as they learn how to use the technology. It requires patience.

There is a concept of the medical model of disability versus the social model. The medical model says that a person's disability is the problem. That there is something wrong with the person that needs to be fixed, made whole, or cured. The social model says that the actual problem is an ableist and inaccessible society that is set up by and for nondisabled people, that it is society that needs to be repaired. Or maybe even, our society needs to be "cured" for not caring about and prioritizing making itself accessible to everyone. What if instead of the insistence that those who cannot speak must be stupid, and seeing a nonspeaking autistic person's inability to talk as the problem, we considered the actual problem to be our society's refusal to accept and validate alternative forms of communication? Do you think that Stephen Hawking was stupid, since he could only talk by using a machine? Of course not! You recognize that he is one of the greatest intellects in modern history while also being unable to talk. Please extend that same understanding to autistic people with aphasia. As for me, I would so much rather have an intellectual disability and be kind and ethical than be supposedly "smart" and yet still cruel and selfish. There are many things, dear reader, I hope you take from this book, and one is that you decide today to make an effort to stop saying "dumb" when you actually mean to say "stupid." Do it for childhood Mickey, who knew what everyone else was saying, knew that he couldn't speak, but knew that he wanted to communicate and find human connection and was determined to do so.

Out of this determination I invented my own incredibly detailed sign language with which to communicate. Obviously, this wasn't ideal, but it at least allowed me to scrape by when with my immediate family, who despite any despair over my inability to talk were fairly familiar with my signs. Once I signed asking for an ice cream cone and as soon as I got it, I promptly squished it into my beloved grandmother's face, my attempt at "sharing" it with her. Stories like that are a common thread throughout my life. Reaching for human connection, trying to make a moment of friendship and love, but not quite pulling it off. My made-up sign language was a desperate reach to connect with the world, and yet I remained cut off from communication with anyone outside of my immediate family.

In addition to signing, I was stimming. This is the name for the repetitive motions like rocking or flapping that many people associate with autism. While stimming often puzzles or even alarms nonautistic people, autistic people know it to be calming and regulating. When external stimulus outside of our control is too overwhelming, perhaps an air conditioner buzzing like an angry dislodged hive, it feels incredibly helpful to give ourselves sensory input that we *can* control. This isn't actually an unfamiliar concept to nonautistic people. If you're nonautistic and have ever wrung your hands when feeling anxious, congratulations! You just stimmed. Autistic people might do such things more often or in ways that seem more visibly obvious and seemingly less acceptable, but at its core stimming is something common to all human beings.

I stimmed a lot as a child. I was often rocking back and forth, and I especially enjoyed the sensation of spinning or swinging from a rope. If ever I felt particularly upset or frustrated, it felt helpful to try to throw my tiny frame down to the ground as hard as I could. I know this is difficult for nonautistic people to make sense of, but believe me when I say that it was the most calming and regulating thing I could do for myself in the moment. To block out the uncontrollable sensory input coming from outside me with the forceful, *controllable*, proprioceptive *woosh smash*. This is what me calming myself down and regulating my input can look like. The bigger the sensory input outside of me, the bigger the self-stimulation that is needed to mask it.

When an autistic child is flapping their arms or rocking back and forth, they don't secretly wish they could stop flapping or rocking; they are flapping and rocking to self-regulate. It is healthy. May we all learn to regulate ourselves so well. May we all learn what our bodies need to feel calm, safe, and at peace with a world that is out of control. May we all learn what helps us focus in the best possible way. If an autistic person knows they focus best while pacing, flapping their arms, or rocking slightly . . . *great*! Knowledge is the first step to learning that our differences are our strengths.

I know now that I was born too early for my eyes to have fully developed. However, when as a child I was taken in to see doctors and ophthalmologists, they said it wasn't that I couldn't see the pictures but likely that I just didn't understand the exercise or wasn't cooperating. Those doctors either weren't made aware that I was autistic, or they didn't think it was relevant to their assessment. This meant that I received no early intervention for my eyesight. There is a window within which a child's eyes can improve over time if given tools like glasses, and where the muscles and nerves in a child's eye develop and learn to focus. For me, that window was allowed to silently close and lock, the key carelessly dropped and forever lost.

When I was five, every night before bed, a book about a sizable gray whale was read to me. I remember peppering my mom with questions about this mysterious skill that I knew other people had. At what age can you read? How does it work? How old do you have to be before the symbols of the words appear on the page for you? She was impatient to get back to finishing the book, so I was left unsatisfied, not knowing much more than I did before. What I knew was that the pages just looked blank to me. I could see a blurry rectangle of white, but the page was only white, blank and white; the words just weren't there. I could see where there were smears of color on some of the pages: rough, fuzzy, indistinct shapes. Rocks, I supposed. But that was it.

When I was six, I finally received my first pair of glasses. They had red frames and flexible earpieces that curled all the way around my ears so I could bounce, and spin, and stim without them falling off. It was incredibly disorienting to experience slightly clearer vision. Now with my glasses I could see the world more like the average person, but just blurred as if I was looking through a thick Vaseline-like filter or like looking down a long, distorted carnival fun house tunnel.

While still far from 20/20 vision, this was a major improvement. I remember standing in the optometrist's office, managing to cope by focusing on just one thing at a time. I was utterly transfixed as I stared out the window at a tree. For the first time in my life I could see there were many separate pieces making up the tree. Before that, trees looked to me like how a very small child would draw one: a brown stick with a fuzzy green cloud on top. This was an incredibly overwhelming amount of sensory input. I lay sick on my back on the grass under a tree in my yard for two days, the pokey grass providing a positive sensory input to help elevate the sickening movement of the leaves and light above.

Eventually, I was eager to truly see my whale book. I was delighted to discover that what I had always thought was a picture of a rock was actually a picture of the very hefty whale! Although he had swum through my bedroom every night for years, I felt like in that moment I instantly knew that whale so much more than I ever did before; I thought that *this* must be what it's like to make a friend.

3

"Come to the edge" he said,
"We can't, we are afraid" they said. . . .
"Come to the edge"
"We can't, we will fall"
"Come to the edge"
and they came
and he pushed them
and they flew.

—Guillaume Apollinaire

Over time I was joined by two younger brothers, who were both born full term to a somewhat more experienced mother. It quickly became evident that they were much preferred over me. I was frequently left feeling wounded and given up on when my mom would openly say dismissive things about me to her friends like, "The first pancake never turns out." Remember, even when I couldn't talk, I still heard and understood everything. My mom said to me once, "I'm not happy when I'm near you. You aren't happy. If you were just somewhere else, we would both be happier." I wonder if she had any quiet concern that I might actually be able to understand what she was saying. That I might actually see her. I suppose she was scared, maybe sad or frustrated. Perhaps she was actually more disappointed in herself as a mother than she was in me as a son. She didn't have the ending to the book yet. She didn't have a story like this to show her that she didn't have to be scared, that autism comes with both weaknesses and strengths, that knowledge is power and that there is a place for everyone in this world.

My mother began sending me to live with her parents for long periods of time rather than juggle a growing family and a son who struggled to communicate with the world. Despite the trauma of rejection by my own mother, living with my grandparents was in many ways a wonderful change for me.

Gramps had a tiny tin rowboat with an outboard motor and would go fishing for salmon every day. If ever the Coast Guard gave him a hard time, he would fake senility until they gave up and let him get back to it. He had a little garden shed he had turned into a cold smoker and would smoke the twenty-pound salmon he had caught into lox. After he cleaned the fish, he would throw the parts of the salmon he didn't want onto the beach, and bald eagles would swoop down and pick them up. Though the fish innards were disgusting, oily, and smelly, the eagles swooping down were fascinating: not even stopping to land, just swooping low enough to ground to seize the innards in their talons midflight.

Just as with the eagles, I remember being equal parts fascinated and disgusted by the way Gramps consumed cheese. He would cut a large slab of cheddar cheese, plate it, and microwave it until it was a gooey and stretchy mess, somehow both a mound and puddled at the same time. He'd then spin its greasy threads around his fork before mashing the strings in his mouth. Before retirement he had been both a doctor and a lawyer and now spent his days in the rowboat or playing solitaire on his computer with a veracity I could only assume meant he was training for the Olympic solitaire team. Although he was kind, he also had the forceful arrogance that comes from having existed at the pinnacle of privilege. Casual racism and misogyny was just part of his worldview. His medical specialty had been gynecology. I wonder if women believing they had to be completely dependent on his expertise just fit cleanly into how he believed the greater world should work when it came to interactions between men and women.

Despite that, it was clear to all that Geema wore the pants—a true, strong matriarch of the family. She held this position at the head of our extended family not through manipulation or control, but by being a force of enveloping warmth and kindness. Her tiny frame was always rippling with laughter, lit up by a radiant smile. She had abundant patience for me touching the tips of her short, gray, bristly hair whenever she picked me up. She made a game out of everything, like the time she lost her acrylic nail in a cake she was baking. She informed the table that whoever found her acrylic nail would get a prize, before bursting into peals of sharp laughter. She was like a wind chime, releasing a musical "ha-ha-ha" with every breeze of joy she found in life.

Ours was a Jewish family, but I liked to think of us as "Jewish with an emphasis on the ish." Like a cat with a belled collar, you always knew where in the house Geema was because of the constant sputtering of half-Yiddish sounds. "Oy-yoy-yoy-yoy" and "prettttyyy good . . . pretty pretty pretty pretty good" were the music underscoring my life in her home, long before it was popularized by a similarly Jewish-ish character on the HBO TV show *Curb Your Enthusiasm*.

She was part of a group called "The Crazy Ladies Ski Bus," which to me seemed equal parts amazing adventure and fanatic cult: a vibrant society of perpetually laughing old ladies who would ride up to the mountains surrounding Seattle and ski down the steep, cliff-faced moguls of the double black diamonds. She had found her people and made it a priority to spend as much time with them as possible. I remember her being undaunted by repeated battles with cancer, getting chemotherapy one day and skiing with the Crazy Ladies the next. She raced in her first triathlon when she was eighty, coming in first in her age group—also, the *only* person in her age group. I remember hoping that one day I might have adventures as exciting and death defying as hers.

Geema was unstoppable, and even her casually misogynistic husband respected it as an immutable law of the universe. A little engine of woman barreling down the track sounding her whistle of "oys" and "ha-has" or "preeettty pretty goods." You had to either get on board or get out of the way. If there was something she wanted to do, she didn't talk about it. She just did it. This included the way she loved me, the rejected firstborn grandson who could neither see nor communicate clearly. Geema was real with me and loved that I was real and genuine with her. She believed I was capable of so much more than anyone else gave me credit for, and she would push me accordingly. Geema kayaked, and so I wanted to as well. She insisted that if I wanted to kayak, then I first needed to learn Eskimo rolls. She would get me situated in the kayak then flip it over, forcing me to have to right it while upside down and underneath the surface of the icy, salty water. If I wanted to kayak, then she wanted to walk me through the steps required for me to do it safely and independently. She was the first person, and for many years the only person, who believed that I was inherently capable. She was the only person whose voice didn't change when she talked to me. She was just always herself. Always real. She was such a healing balm for me during this time.

Much of my childhood I lived alone in my thoughts, in my dreams, in my own imaginary worlds. My grandparents' home backed onto a West Seattle beach, and it was the perfect environment for my imagination to really flourish. Despite America's glorification of rigorous academics, early literacy, and multitudes of tests, there is a wealth of research from across the world that tells us that unstructured play is even more crucial and beneficial for the development of young children, with boredom being the birthplace of creativity. This was exactly the kind of environment my grandparents cultivated for me.

Gramps built me a two-story pirate ship out of wood pallets and anchored it with a long rope chained off to a log so I could float all around by the ferry dock in West Seattle. I imagined myself to be menacing the lumbering ferry boats with my swift and deadly ship. I had a plank, ladders up to the mast, with a skull and crossbones fiercely fluttering in the salty Puget Sound breeze. My nose filled with the smell of windblown salt and seaweed. I spent years as a pirate, sailing the Salish Sea and becoming well acquainted with Pacific Northwest marine life. I marveled at the rough sandpaper of starfish, the playful otters that dared to poop on my fearsome pirate poop deck, and every so often the occasional baby octopus! I learned the hard way that they are small but mighty, and they bite with a tiny parrot-like beak hidden at the meeting of their tentacles. I relished in every moment of animal encounter. My fellow humans seemed so obsessed with me learning to communicate in a way that was convenient for them, but the sea animals didn't make speaking a requirement for interaction with me. They already understood.

For all these reasons it was *a pirate's life for me, yo-ho-ho*. Autistic people are, after all, better set up for success when they have clear roles, titles, and job descriptions. When you are acting, you always have a clear character. This is why autistic kids often love wearing costumes, superhero capes, pirate hats, or clown noses. It gives them a specific lens with which to interact with the world. It tells them how to behave. *If you didn't have that specific role, how would you know how you were supposed to act in that moment?* Being a pirate made it so that I knew what I was supposed to do in any given moment. I knew how I was supposed to act and what I was supposed to do, because I'd witnessed it being done in movies, in books, and on TV. If I was just Mickey, what was that role? What is a Mickey supposed to do in any given situation? I didn't know! I couldn't intuit those things like nonautistic kids. *But a pirate?* That, I knew. That was a lens I could use.

Right now, this interaction with you, my friend, is so easy. I am the writer; you are the reader. You flip the pages, and I am supposed to sound smart. Funny? Yes, smart and funny. The roles are incredibly clear. If we were peers and passed each other unexpectedly on the street, though, those roles aren't as clear. How are we supposed to interact then? Not as doctor and patient, barista and customer, but as peers? Where are the rules? Where is the handbook? There are no roles that say here is how I am supposed to act and here is how you are supposed to act.

I also became obsessed with clowns, magicians, and people who I knew got to interact with society by playing a role. I would frequently not go out in public unless I was dressed as a clown. I wore a clown costume to the hospital for my brother's birth so that he would have a clown at his "first" birthday party. Interacting with the world as simply my own self was too difficult. It felt too vulnerable to again and again reach for but ultimately fail at human interaction. Ironically, isn't this the essence of clowns, who try again and again and again but fail again and again, all the while wishing and reaching for human connection?

My grandparents never made me feel like I had to be anything other than exactly who I was. They never pushed me to act more neurotypical. They instead did a wonderful job of encouraging me to pursue the ways in which I did feel comfortable interacting with the world. If I felt more comfortable going out as a clown, they simply celebrated both my love of clowns and willingness to venture out into the world. They trusted that when I was ready, I'd move on from it, but until that day they'd be all for it.

Once, Geema found me on my belly in my room, feet swinging behind me as I drew pictures of clowns. She then threw herself into making my creations into wearable pieces for me. They were often variations of a similar design: a boxy shirt and pants, with big frills at my wrists and ankles. She would take me to scour fabric stores with her, looking for the printed fabric that most closely resembled whatever fantastical design I had imagined. She would ball yarn into giant pom-poms, with three of them running down the shirt, like a circus snowman. It was our tradition well into my high school years. I would draw sketches of the costumes, and she would sew them. She sewed on her machines in her "booby trap room," where she said you had to be very careful where you stepped and what you touched, lest a booby trap be set off! I imagined blow darts primed with sewing needles peeking out from behind the closet door, ready to deal me a thousand punctures if I disturbed a surreptitiously trip-wired foot pedal! I steered clear of her sewing studio.

My grandpa would journey down with me into the lower basement levels of the Pike Place Market to the aptly named Pike Place Market Magic Shop.

Old magic posters were pasted on the shop exterior, and stepping inside was like tumbling into a wonderland. It seemed that every inch of available wall space had an item for sale. There were card sets, props, and books galore, and every time we went, I saw a few more things I'd never seen before.

Although it was at least quieter than the heaving tourist attraction above, there was a parade of painted props, feathered boas, and sensory input everywhere I looked . . . and I loved it. I especially coveted the knowledge tucked away in the Tarbell Course in Magic series. The Tarbell Books are an eight-part encyclopedia of magic written one hundred years ago in the 1920s, but they have stood the test of time and are in no way outdated. They detailed nearly every magic trick in existence at the time, and to this day any dazzling "new" trick you see can have its roots traced back to this original, premier magic resource. I was especially drawn to its large photo diagrams that meant that one did not need to be able to read the small-print words to understand how the tricks were done.

Gramps noticed the way I lingered over the weighty tomes each time we went to the magic shop, and so he began a tradition of purchasing the next book in the set for me on every birthday.

But perhaps the most inadvertently life-changing thing they gave me was this: Geema got a subscription to Seattle Children's Theatre, a professional theatre for young audiences. I remember the first time I walked into the big, colorful building, tightly clutching the glossy paper tickets that she gave me the responsibility of holding. She prompted me to hand them to someone who worked at the theatre, who then gave back my tickets, but this time with the ends snapped off. I ran my thumb along on the newly rough edge of my shortened tickets as we walked farther into the cavernous lobby, and I took in my surroundings.

All around us were other children with their grown-ups, chattering with each other so easily. I held tighter to Geema's hand, and she squeezed back. It's a simple gesture that is calming to many a nonautistic kid, but that proprioceptive input was especially reassuring to me. Geema shepherded me into our seats, and I looked all around the space, still running my thumb along the rough ticket edge. I noticed clunky cannons hanging up above me and thought to myself that that's what my pirate ship needed next. Then the room faded to brief darkness before the cannons lit up, firing bright beams of light at the stage. Today I know them as Fresnel lanterns. The show began, and the stage filled with color and movement, sound and joy. My world erupted with possibility.

In addition to the comfort of sitting safely in the dark, I got to experience social interactions from a passive yet shared lens. These actors were showing me human, wise, and flawed characters. It was so freeing to be allowed to witness—from a distance—those messy, social, human-to-human relationships. I was heartened to see actors interacting with the world by playing a character instead of being themselves, just like I did every day.

Sitting on the edge of my seat, I instinctively knew that this was my safe place. This was where I was just as valued as anyone else as an audience member. Although I was in the dark, I finally felt seen, silently heard, and understood. Just like when I was with the sea animals of Puget Sound, me speaking clearly wasn't a requirement for being engaged with. When actors addressed the audience from the stage, and thus me, they didn't change their voice to talk down to me. They were real. They were human. They were honest. All good actors are honest.

The play was *Jack and the Beanstalk*, and the giant was enormous, towering, sky high. In that moment my chest rose, my chin lifted, the corner of my eyes suddenly crinkled, and a parabola stretched across my face. Jack's beanstalk stretched high into the sky, and so did my hopes for myself.

4

*People often become what they believe themselves to be. If I
believe I cannot do something, it makes me incapable of doing it. But when I believe I can, then I acquire the ability to
do it even if I didn't have it in the beginning.*

—Mahatma Gandhi

When I was four, I began speaking, although far from clearly or flu-
ently. At age six, I was in elementary school but my teachers couldn't
understand anything I said. While my family understood my speech, my
teachers couldn't, so I started speech therapy. The therapist manhandled
my tongue, teaching it where in my mouth to sit for different sounds. Forcing my mouth into the proper shapes to make the proper sounds. Stretching
my tongue. I remember being utterly terrified. My tongue felt as if all manner of medieval torture devices had assailed my gagging, gasping mouth. I
remember how much my tongue hurt and how exhausted I was. I endured
four years of this before enough was enough and it truly clicked for me.

Six years old was also when I received my first pair of glasses. They
didn't necessarily make things clearer, but just much larger, like giant magnifying glasses, or the large-print text I would later learn to use. Similarly,
the glasses also enlarged my eyes for other people looking at me from the
outside, like two giant fishbowls in front of my eyes. I looked like a praying
mantis while wearing my glasses: my tiny twig of a frame and my magnified
bug eyes staring out behind the thick lenses. Because of the way my eyes
worked, it seemed that my glasses always had a slight layer of petroleum

jelly on them that I was attempting to look through, no matter what the prescription was or how many times I had cleaned the lenses. Because of this I couldn't complete my schoolwork—not because I wasn't smart enough to do the work, but because I couldn't read the worksheets. But my parents didn't publicize my autism diagnosis, and since I was wearing glasses, no one believed that my eyesight was a problem anymore. It was instead decided that I was just not a smart kid. I had come so far and worked so hard only to end up labeled stupid. I had battled my way out of being nonspeaking, first by developing my own sign language and then, when that wasn't satisfactory for the nonautistic world, submitting to countless hours of agonizing speech therapy so I could learn to communicate in the way that was most comfortable for them. I had spent so long being unable to see, denied glasses for six years. Then when I could see, I remember looking in the mirror and seeing a scrawny wisp of a boy, with larger-than-life eyes peering back at him. I saw a large, hooked nose that looked like my father's, his nose that was mocked nearly daily by my mother. I may have been legally blind, but I could still see so clearly all that disgusted my mother and left her disappointed to have ever given birth to me.

It makes sense that I was desperately grateful to have by then identified my safe havens. My insistence on dressing as a clown teamed with my love of Seattle Children's Theatre performances led to a passion for all things circus. It became a true lifeline for me. I didn't have any friends, but that left me with plenty of time to practice juggling three balls, then four balls, then clubs. My teachers and family all thought I was hopelessly stupid, and yet I was learning skill after skill after difficult skill. I was obsessed. For my ninth birthday I received the six-foot-tall giraffe unicycle I'd been asking for every day for a year. I was stilt walking at every opportunity I could, showing up to town fairs and festivals in costume and on stilts pretending like I had been hired to be there, interacting with people in a way that I never could in my real life. I wasn't interacting with the world as Mickey. I was in costume and was a specific character with a specific role. A giant "professional" stilt walker. Mickey, on the other hand, was tiny, had no friends nor the intuited knowledge of how to make one, and was apparently incredibly dim.

But when I stilt walked, I was as tall as Jack's giant and scores of fairgoers were delighted by my presence, continually expressing their amazement that someone *so* young could be so incredibly talented on stilts. I may not have been interacting with the world as my true self, but I was interacting with the world, and that was some sort of progress. I could feel my strengths growing even then, and I was becoming less ashamed of my differences.

After just showing up at countless fairs and pretending like I was supposed to be there, one year two towering professional stilt walkers at a local fair were surprised to see another stilt walker already there, on their turf! They started trampling toward me, while at the same time looking for the event manager to figure out what was going on. Hadn't their contract rider insisted they would be the only stilt walkers at this event? When they realized I was only nine and started talking to me, they caught on. I saw their shoulders relax. I was on tall wooden peg stilts that required constant tiny steps to keep balanced. Forward. Backward. Forward. Backward. Forward. Backward. They were on state-of-the-art articulated bigfoot stilts used by Disneyland and Universal Studios. "What's wrong, kid? You have to pee?" the slicker of the two stilt walkers snickered. I tried to explain, but the taller of the stripe-suited men insisted, "I know, I know, peg stilts, only joking! Jeez!"

These carnies took me under their wing. They walked with me all day, and spent their breaks telling me the ins and outs of stilt walking. How to get my costumes made. What kind of stilts to wear at which events. How to deal with hecklers. This was the most real human interaction with someone outside of my family that this nine-year-old had ever gotten. One was a grease-polished, streamlined used car salesman of a man. The other one was a little off looking. A warm, smiling mensch with a facial difference on his nose. The latter was the nicer of the two. Both were towering in striped pants. Both were genuinely interested in me and interested in encouraging my passion. This was uncharted territory for me, but I was determined to not let this opportunity pass me by. I peppered them with questions and made mental note of things they could do on their towering stilts that I would go home and practice till I had it mastered.

Back at school, despite the weighty glasses that continually dragged themselves down my nose, I was still unable to see clearly enough to read. My teachers were quick to give up on me to focus their energies on educating the kids who responded well to the ways in which they taught. Rarely did anyone try to think up an out-of-the-box teaching strategy that would work for me, instead leaving me to figure out how to provide for myself, make my own accommodations. I had to skip most recesses because the schoolwork and reading took me so long that I could not complete it during regular class time. My nonautistic peers solidified friend circles out on the playground while I desperately squinted at the pages, willing the words to emerge into legibility for me. Was it any wonder I didn't have any friends? Because I was both low vision and autistic, I just couldn't win at the making friends game.

I was either inside still staring at papers they had breezed through earlier, or when I did go to recess, I would just pace, waiting for the recess time to end or talk to the playground duty. Autistics are very good at pacing.

In the middle of another painstaking fifth-grade day, in the middle of yet another exam I could barely read, the class time ended and my classmates bustled out to recess, chattering among themselves brightly and with a confidence that pissed me off. Looking at her last remaining student's spindly frame still hunched over the desk, knowing that he assumed he couldn't leave until the test was completed, Miss Ritchie had an idea. She sent me to recess to pace even though my exam hadn't been completed yet. This was new! When I returned, there was something else even more outlandish. There was a giant 11″ × 17″ photocopy of the exam on my desk. Miss Ritchie said she had a hunch that if the text were just larger, I might be able to read it. It took me less than ten minutes to complete the second half of the test. The first half had taken well over an hour and change. It was a revelation. For the first time in my life I could truly read.

Miss Ritchie then fought to get me an individualized education program, better known as an IEP. It is a legal document that is developed for each public school child in the U.S. who needs special education, to ensure that they will receive the reasonable accommodations they need to be able to access a public school education. Unfortunately, this was ultimately only a symbolic victory. Even though an IEP had been secured and even though my accommodation was easy, things didn't necessarily get easier. Throughout the rest of my schooling my teachers were just lazy, even though the Americans with Disabilities Act required them to provide me with large-print tests. My necessary accommodation was so easy. Either photocopy worksheets onto 11″ × 17″ paper, or open in Word, select all, change the font size to eighteen, and click Print. It took minutes and cost pennies. Often teachers in middle school, high school, and college would tell me that they would be giving me an unfair advantage by giving me large-print materials. They didn't see it as leveling the playing field so a disabled kid could have the same opportunities as the nondisabled kids. They saw it as giving the disabled kid an unfair advantage over the nondisabled kids. Did they neither see nor care that the nondisabled kids already had advantages over me in nearly every other aspect of life? All I needed was large print!

Meanwhile in my safe havens, the Seattle Opera had been looking for a stilt walker to play an ostrich for *The Magic Flute* by Wolfgang Amadeus Mozart. My eleven-year-old life was stilt walking, and since people knew my obsession, I found out about the audition. I showed up to the audition, just like I had been showing up to county fairs for years. I brought no resume nor headshot, but I did bring the stilts that I had made myself. Turns out the ostrich costume weighed fifty pounds. I weighed fifty pounds. I didn't get the part. The slicked-back used car salesman of a stilt walker from the fair the year before was also at the audition. I bet he got the part. He definitely weighed more than fifty pounds. But I guess they took a liking to this plucky kid, even though he didn't say much or make eye contact. They asked me to be in their next show as a street urchin. It was going to be my turn to be on a stage, just like Jack and his beanstalk had been years before! When you aren't distracted by social rules, there isn't anything you can't do. While the other kids at school made friend circles that I just couldn't figure out how to break into, I spent that alone time practicing magic and circus skills. And when my peers went home after school to read books or play Nintendo with their friends, I was off to the Seattle Opera House to act in a professional opera production.

Middle school started, and I was in special ed for more of the day now. The room consisted of people with Down syndrome, autism, d/Deaf students, and students in wheelchairs . . . which Lord knows why they needed special ed. A room full of the disabled kids who had been branded as, to quote Steve Jobs, "the crazy ones. The misfits. The rebels. The trouble-makers. The round pegs in the square holes. The ones who see things differently. The ones who are not fond of rules and have no respect for the status quo."

In the back of the room were all of my large-print books, since they were too heavy for me to keep in my backpack and too bulky to even all fit in my locker. I was still incredibly small for my age, a preemie who'd never managed to catch up in size, but had so many items surrounding me anytime I needed to read. I had dome-shaped magnifying glasses that I would move around my pages. My backpack bulged with $11'' \times 17''$ photocopies of tests and exams, all folded in half so they'd fit in my bag. Tapes from the talking book and braille library. There was a giant machine built in the eighties that included a slide tray for a book, a camera, and the oldest-looking monitor I have ever seen. It displayed large-print, color-reversed versions of the text that was put under it: eighteen-point font, light green text on a black background. All of these pieces of equipment were to help me read.

I spent the next four years at the Seattle Opera in performances such as *The Barber of Seville*, *Falstaff*, and *I Puritani*. I would spend my time back-stage listening to the orchestra, keeping my hands busy with my rust-colored costume hat. I would marvel at the way the old felt wool fuzzed against my fingertips. I'd be tossing it in the air, rolling it down my arm, catching it on my head, and practicing juggling with this dusty opera relic. I was always moving as much as possible backstage, before I had to be onstage standing perfectly still while waiting for the particular beat of music that would command me into movement.

While they were often nonspeaking roles, I did get to sing as an altar boy in *Tosca*. By day I was singing, practicing for my bar mitzvah, and at night I was singing on the Seattle Opera stage in a Catholic robe.

I finally got to bust out my beloved stilts in two different productions of *La Bohème*. I would lead a marching band down a flight of stairs while on stilts and waving a *giant* French flag. These stairs were built by the Metropolitan Opera in the eighties, had toured the world in a truck, been unloaded in countless cities, and used forced perspective to make the stage look even bigger than it was. This means they were very wobbly, and while the rise of the stairs was similar to a traditional stair, the part where you put your foot (the run) was much smaller. I always secretly eyed the largest bass singer I could find to cushion my landing if I were to fall.

My wildest of all dreams came true when I was cast in the seafaring adventure opera *Billy Budd*. Reflecting on this as an adult, I realize that my role was that of a British sailor, but at the time I was convinced I was playing a pirate! This is what I'd spent years training for out on the water behind my grandparents' home, and now I could show the world my skills! I was climbing up the ropes, sitting on top of the mast, and crawling through the trapdoors on a smoke-and-haze-filled stage in front of thousands of people every night. The makeup team would pat my face, nose, eyes, and chest with grease, char, and sticky glycerin artificial sweat, which was almost unbearable for a child on the spectrum, but I tolerated it as the trade-off necessary to get to pretend to be a real pirate night after night.

Like I said, a lot of this experience could have been unbearable for a child on the spectrum. While you are onstage, there are often bright lights shining on you and loud noises that erupt from all kinds of places. However, you've rehearsed all these things in advance and you know where each sound and light cue is happening because it happens in the exact same place every single night, so it almost feels like you are in control of those things. Knowing what to expect makes you feel like you are in on the magic, and we all know how I felt about magic.

The most important part of being an actor is to be a living, breathing, listening person, and on this ship, I was *living*! Representation matters, and it was also meaningful to me to take in the story of Billy Budd every night.

Here was a handsome leading character of an opera, who had all kinds of swashbuckling adventures even though he had a disability, a stutter. While the speech impediment ultimately led to his death by hanging (*why are operas always so morbid?*), I was so starved of representation that I would take *any* character I could look up to who also had a hard time speaking. *Billy Budd* was truly such a dream come true for me: playing a pirate every night, telling thousands of people a story about a talented sailor who just couldn't talk like everyone else. I grew up backstage at the Seattle Opera among the ropes and dusty pulleys.

Meanwhile at school, I still didn't have any friends. In middle school I went through a few months where I had gotten so bored with pacing the hallways for years and wanted so badly to be a good person and make a friend that I held the door open for literally everyone during lunch. For my entire lunch period I stood at the door that led from our cafeteria to the rest of our school, and every time I saw someone coming, I would open the door for them, like the doorman at an expensive hotel. There would be times when rushes of fifty kids would be going through the door all at once between classes and I would just hold the door open, unflinchingly, for the whole stampede of students while doing my best to give each one of them a Very Good Smile. I was trying extremely hard. To make a connection. To be a good person. To make a friend. But the world hates people who are not socially intelligent, often thinking that social intelligence and kindness are the same thing. They are not. The world loves to believe that someone is either intelligent or they aren't, failing to see that we are all geniuses at something. Every single person on this earth is a genius at something. We can each learn something from everyone else. Even our enemies.

I was always told I "lacked empathy." That all autistic people "lack empathy." And yet here I was going out of my way to make other people's lives easier for them in the only way I could think to do it, holding the door open for as many people as I possibly could. Yet most of those people couldn't even manage to look at me with a genuine smile while I did it or say thank you. But go ahead, tell me again how I'm the one who lacks empathy.

I remember once in school someone asked if they could borrow a pencil. I felt warm and tingly all over! *That was it! That was human interaction with a peer! I had done it!* I replied with a dry, "Sure," but inwardly I was elated. Raging teenage hormones, the mystery of an aloof man, or maybe a bit of both made it so that despite my uncertainty with how to handle social situations, girls would still initiate interaction with me. I remember girls would flirt with me or groups of girls would sometimes say, "Hi Mickey," when I walked down the hallway, but I didn't reply. I didn't even realize that I should say hi back. Instead, I held my arms from my shoulders all the way down to my fingers pointed stiffly down toward the floor to make sure I wasn't fidgeting. I wasn't trying to be rude. I just couldn't intuit what was expected of me in that interaction. Were they flirting with me or mocking me? I still don't know, because I only remember it from the perspective of an autistic teenager who still hadn't figured out how to make friends.

But autistic people want friends and human interaction just as much as anyone else. We can be thrilled just passively participating, simply standing in the circle while everyone else talks! It's much like my world was rocked just sitting in the dark at the theatre, watching the actors perform human interaction for me to analyze. It's an isolating misconception that we autistics don't want friends or that we always want to be alone. It's not that we don't want friends, it's just that we don't instinctively know how to make friends, and few nondisabled people instinctively know how to make friends with a disabled person.

I remember the exact day in middle school I figured out that "small talk" wasn't always that mysterious. I did this by realizing that nearly every conversation I had during the day was a repeating pattern. The exact same four sentences split between two people, repeated again and again and again, like a script in a play.

"Hi. How are you doing today?"

"Pretty good. How 'bout you?"

These four sentences made up nearly every conversation.

"Hi. How are you doing today?"

"Pretty good. How 'bout you?"

I could learn this. I could learn this script.

Unfortunately, while I frequently lived at my grandma's house, I also frequently lived at my mom's house. My mom, Sandy, felt to me like a facade on a facade. I felt like she was more interested in the image of herself that she presented to her friends on one of her silver-plated platters than she was in the reality of how she acted when her friends weren't watching. Her hair was dyed black and cropped into a short bob, and it made her look a lot like Liza Minelli. She had used an unnatural voice when she spoke to nonspeaking me years before but also used a different unnatural voice when talking to nearly everyone. While complaining to waiters she would use a very sweet voice. The words she was saying while demanding her Starbucks coffee be hotter or Olive Garden meal be taken back and replaced were very unkind and rude, but the tone of her voice was sweet and she was smiling. Didn't she know it only made her seem meaner that she smiled while being rude to these people? I truly don't think she knew. Wouldn't the customer service people appreciate it more if she was genuine?

I believe we should always be nice to customer service people, but the nice should be genuine. Nonautistic people think they are so good at acting. But the real secret of acting is not to act at all, but to be genuine and live. Nonautistic people are somehow able to manage to be confusing while also being so transparent. Maybe because autistic people have to work so hard to pass as neurotypical, we also analyze and see through all the social baloney. When my brothers visited my grandparents, they were not themselves. They were overly polite. They didn't talk about anything real, anything that excited them. They were so polite and sterile and unhuman that my grandmother never really got to know them. If you really loved someone, wouldn't you want to just be yourself so that person could know the real you and what you thought? My brothers thought if you loved someone you should act the way that you imagine they want you to act, instead of really loving them and really being loved by letting them see the real you.

My mother loved playing social games. And I didn't know how to play social games. I couldn't. I was only interested in living my life. I didn't have time for social games. So my mother would discipline me with social games. When my brothers beat me up, punching the air out of my chest and even once punching the contact lens out of my eye, they would be rewarded with hugs and kisses, and I would be sent to my room. One of my brothers had a pneumatic air compressor that one would use for construction tools like nail guns. He was quite the tinkerer and always building things. Using valves and PVC pipes, he built an air gun that he would use to shoot rocks and pebbles through the wooden fence in our backyard. He assured me frequently that one day he was going to sneak into my room at night and shoot me in the head with it. The violence from my brothers continued well into college. Whenever I was being physically hurt by someone, I made a pact with God, like there was some big universal trial going on, or to show my mother that I wasn't actually a bad person like she thought. I made a pact to never do anything wrong and that if I was being hurt, I would never physically hurt the person back. I would just curl into a ball and take it. Surely if I always responded with a refusal to hit back, my mom, or *someone*, would change their mind and realize that I wasn't a bad person. Realize what was going on was not okay. I would frequently tell my brothers that I didn't blame them for what they were doing to me. That it wasn't their fault that our family was hurtful and dysfunctional, but that it didn't make it okay. Nothing changed.

But why would they change? Sometimes I was disgusted by my brothers. By the parts of them that I wanted to feel different from. By the parts of them that I worked so hard to be the opposite of. But I suppose that's exactly how they felt about me as well, so how could one have hard feelings about that? Live and let live, I suppose.

Despite this family life that made my stomach churn like a hair-raising roller-coaster ride, all was still progressing rapidly over in my safe havens. My first part-time job during high school involved turning my hobby into income and being hired to perform in magic shows for birthday parties, synagogues, and even for the annual Optometrists of America meeting. Before then I'd been making fifty dollars per show, but these optometrists paid me one hundred dollars! Any money I made went right back into my circus skills. I heard about Chris Holm, a professional unicycler who lived a few hours north of me in Vancouver. He became the pioneer of mountain unicycling, and I wanted to be a part of it. I watched videos of Chris Holm unicycling down wobbly bridges in the forest, hopping over roots and rocks, skidding down the side of mountains. All on a unicycle. Surely one tired guy. I knew that I had to try this next. My sensory-seeking nature and need for proprioceptive input craved it. I took one of my unicycles to a mountain bike shop, gave them my magic show money, and had them figure out how to retrofit it with a BMX tire.

I managed to get the attention of my unicycling hero Chris Holm when he was in town for a unicycling convention, and he let me come mountain unicycling with him and learn the ropes for an afternoon. I unicycled down mountains in Canada, Washington, and Colorado. Each time the mountain rangers were hesitant to let a unicyclist take the chairlift up and ride down the bike paths, but I was determined and not to be deterred. Each time I offered that one of their rangers could ride up with me the first time, see my skill, and decide after that. They agreed, and every single time I was ultimately given the all clear.

There are so many amazing mountains in the Pacific Northwest, including active volcanoes like Mount Rainier and Mount Saint Helens. Now, it's common knowledge that Everest is the highest mountain on earth, with a summit at 29,029 feet above sea level. Washington's Mount Rainier seemingly pales in comparison with its summit at 14,411 feet. But Everest also sits perched atop the highest mountain range in the world, with a base elevation of about 17,500 feet. Mount Rainier begins only 1,600 feet above sea level. This means that Everest's height above base is nearly 11,500 feet. Rainier? Just over 12,800. When you take away Everest's head start, suddenly it's not so high and mighty. Also, Mount Rainier is an active volcano, so it's automatically cooler! Everything can always be looked at through a different perspective, and the things that look the highest, the mightiest, and the most accomplished usually just got a massive head start or are standing on the shoulders of others.

As I rode down the rooted and rocky dirt trails, my single wheel spun furiously. It forced my two legs to pedal along with it like a wooden walking duck push toy that becomes a flurry of flapping feet as you push it. Every knobbly root I launched off of, every rock that created a drop, felt like an obstacle course nature had created just for me. Woosh, woosh, bounce, bump, woosh, woosh.

Although I still hadn't figured out how to make a friend, I was still one hell of a unicyclist who had somehow persuaded Chris Holm and park rangers to agree to let me explore the horizons of what was possible on a unicycle. I just couldn't get those skills of persuasion with strangers to translate into lasting connections with my peers or family.

Senior year came, and at that time occupational therapy was the bane of my existence. I hated it even more than speech therapy. My fingers and hands, strong and skilled from countless hours of juggling and sleight-of-hand tricks, ached in seething pain from having to do so much typing in OT. At this point the occupational therapist had me sat at a computer keyboard nearly every day. Typing. "The quick brown fox jumped over the lazy dog. The quick brown fox jumped over the lazy dog." Over and over again. My hands, already wracked with so much tension from autism, spasmed and pulsed by the end of each session. I hated it. Why would anyone ever want to type their thoughts? I swore I would never type that many words again. "The quick brown fox." It's not like I'd choose to do something stupid and write a book or anything like that. (I think the irony of this is hilarious now.)

Anyway, it was time to nail down what I wanted to do after high school, and my instinct was to go study theatre. Performance had been such a confidence-building and life-giving place for me, and I wanted to see how far I could go with it. Funnily enough, while my average grades through school were Ds and Cs, the only class I ever received an F in was drama class in high school. It was a punitive F anyway, as it was given to me because I chose getting paid to perform at Seattle Opera over the extracurricular school spring musical. My love for theatre was kept alive though by my special ed teacher and the school's technical director teaming up to demonstrate their belief in me. Since high school was nearly over anyway, my special ed teacher cut a deal with me. If I showed up for attendance, they would look the other way while I snuck out of the special ed room to go work in the theatre with the technical director, John. He let me help paint sets, hang lights, program the light board, and more. When outside groups rented the school's theatre space and needed to hire someone familiar with the space to handle their tech needs, I was John's recommendation.

I applied for and was accepted into my local college, the University of Washington, with plans to take classes in its drama school. Now, my grades weren't great, but apparently the university was enamored with my entrance essay. In it I told the story of how I'd been entertaining a crowd by juggling knives on a five-foot-tall unicycle when my shoelace got tangled in the chain and gear. I noticed the whole audience gasp before I felt the lace of my Converse high-tops pulling tighter and tighter around my ever-squishing foot. I was now tied to the unicycle so if I were to lose my balance, I wouldn't be able to simply jump off, landing on my feet like I usually would. My foot was tied four feet up the cycle. The audience noticed before I did and was genuinely fearful for me, but I played it up and made it an even more enjoyable performance for them. I jokingly blamed it on the volunteer who had been handing up my juggling knives to me. I looked at them disapprovingly and exclaimed, "May I please have *another* volunteer!" The audience laughed so hard! I handed the second volunteer one of the juggling knives and had them cut loose the lace. That audience felt even more special, even more excited, because they had experienced something that was truly unique and just for them. They had experienced a moment that didn't happen every time I did my show and would likely never happen again. Even though something had gone wrong during the act, it ended up being the best that the routine had ever gone. In life we get the opportunity of seeing everything that happens to us as a gift. We get to make it so that everything that happens to us happens for a reason. We can turn our shoelace lemons into standing ovation lemonade. My little college essay detailing this story allowed me to get into the university even though I had only received Cs and Ds in high school.

At the same time, in a storybook full-circle moment, I was finally cast in a show at Seattle Children's Theatre. I was going back to the place where my world had burst into possibility years before, but this time my role wasn't the audience member passively learning about human interaction. This time I was going to be the actor bringing it all to life!

I had grown up. When you picture an autistic person in your head, you nearly always picture a child. But autistic children grow up into autistic adults. And usually when they do, they disappear. Special ed disappears. They are segregated and exiled into invisibility. They disappear into unemployment. When the national unemployment rate was 4.5 percent, the unemployment rate for autistic college graduates was 85 percent. This is not because we are less talented or skilled, but because of prejudice and assumptions others have before ever even meeting us.

Thank you for reading this book. By reading this book you are meeting us and you are learning more about yourself. My childhood had been a wildly mixed bag of one blow after another, teamed with soaring successes in other areas. But I'd made it through, and I was onto an independent adult life. I felt full of potential and for the first time safely and permanently out of my mother's house. My differences are my strengths, and don't forget, so are yours.

5

I have lived on a razor's edge. So what if you fall off? I'd rather be doing something I really wanted to do. I'd walk it again.

—Georgia O'Keeffe

I'd made it to college, but I made it my mission to leave without the burden of student loan debt. While still in my freshman year at college I'd secured employment performing at Seattle Children's Theatre for three months out of the year, but I was going to need to hustle throughout the other nine months. So I went to the university library, polished and printed my resume, practiced my smile in the library's bathroom mirror trying hard not to be noticed by the other students, and hit the pavement of the outdoor shopping mall that flanked one side of my college campus, teeming with schools of bougie Lululemon stay-at-home mothers living up the next few hours while their kids were at school, as well as the denim-and-flannel-infested restaurant strip that flanked the other side of the campus. I mustered all my people skills and confidently handed in resumes and asked to introduce myself to managers. I applied to as many places as I could, but I couldn't manage to make it past the interview section of my application process. It made no sense to me at the time, but I've realized a lot since then.

The traditional American interview process is inherently exclusionary to people on the autism spectrum. Eye contact and handshakes may have nothing to do with the actual job the interviewee is striving for, and yet society still feels determined that they are one of the most important deciding factors in an interview. Why is this? It only weeds out the incredible untapped autistic workforce and wastes the employer's money on costs associated with high turnover. We know from a survey by the Center for American Progress that the cost of replacing an employee can be double that employee's annual salary.[1]

Autistic people are known to be incredibly loyal employees who strongly value maintaining their employment with one employer for a long time, and it's common for us to fully invest ourselves into whatever our job is. Giving opportunities to autistic people is an out-of-the-box, inclusive, and effective strategy to limit employee turnover. If society could get over its preference for in-person interviews with lots of small talk, eye contact, and firm handshakes and instead consider working interviews where a person gets to demonstrate themselves doing the job that they love doing, then autistic people would be hired a lot more and employers would be very pleased by the results.

With autism comes a new way of thinking: a fresh eye, a fresh mind. Literally, a completely different wiring of the brain. We think differently than most people, so we are amazing problem solvers and innovators. If most people are looking at a problem from one angle, autistic employees are able to see the problem from a completely different perspective. Who wouldn't want to hire that into their organization? All that said, at this moment in 2020 as I write this book, society isn't there yet, and it certainly wasn't there in 2007 as I was rejected again and again after every interview I got a shot at.

By this point you know the unemployment rate for college graduates on the autism spectrum was 85 percent, compared to about 4 percent for everyone else.

Well, I hadn't even graduated from college yet, and there I was, unemployed. I was not going to just accept the fact that I couldn't get past interviews. This wasn't the plan! I was going to graduate debt-free! The same determination that drove me to invent my own sign language years earlier fueled me again, and I decided to take matters into my own hands. If no one would employ me, then I would be self-employed. Sometimes we all need to be our own biggest champions. I decided to throw myself into street performing. I'd be striding around up on my stilts while juggling or twisting balloons into animals on the sidewalk at public markets, all with a hat out hoping for donations. Many people felt this was a roundabout way to try to survive my newfound independence, but the truth of the matter was, it was the only real option I had.

I had no choice but to street perform with my hat out. Had I secured one of those jobs I applied for, I very well may not have even received a paycheck that guaranteed me enough pay to cover my bus transportation, let alone lunch or rent. At the time of writing this, the federal minimum wage is $7.25 per hour, but only if you *don't* have a disability. Segregated just for those lucky few who have disabilities, there is no federal minimum wage. It is up to the employer to decide how little they would like to pay someone with a disability.

At this point in time, for every dollar a white man makes, a white woman makes eighty-one cents, and a Black or Latinx woman makes seventy-five cents. That pay gap absolutely needs to be filled. But meanwhile there are instances in the United States of America where disabled people have been paid as little as three or four cents per hour at major corporations, even though the federal minimum wage is $7.25 per hour. In recent years, there have been reports of an estimated 420,000 individuals with disabilities who have been paid an average of just $2.15 per hour.[2] In Seattle it cost me five dollars in bus fare to ride the bus from my suburb into downtown Seattle, then another five dollars in bus fare to ride the bus back home at the end of the day. That would have been most of my day's pay blown just on bus fare.

So, every employment-related disappointment had led to me making my way through college by busking,[3] which is the fancy word for street performing. And perhaps it was for the best, because I loved it. The hat I put out in front of me always reminded me of the crumpled wool felt relic from the Seattle Opera House. I learned that it is always important to "seed" your hat with a few bills before beginning work to help people tip you. No one wants to be the first to do anything. It is so hard to be the first person to do anything. I learned that people are like sheep: if I put quarters in my hat, they would tip with quarters; if I put dollar bills in my hat before I began, they would tip with dollar bills; if I put a five-dollar bill in my hat, every so often a person would put a five in! I wore wool high-waisted pinstriped trousers, which, at that point had been sewn for me by the Seattle Opera costume shop, along with a white tuxedo shirt, black top hat, and bow tie. I found that people are only comfortable giving money to you if you appear to already have enough money. Maybe this is why we are more comfortable purchasing from corporations than regularly going to a small family-owned business. We know that the corporation already has enough money, but we give them ours anyway because so many other people do, and it feels predictable.

Having spent my four years of college and nearly a decade after that at farmers' markets across the city, I can vividly recall the unique sensation of cobblestones underneath my stilted feet. The smell of fresh fruit, dried flowers, and grilled vegetables kept my spirits floating even higher than the balloons I'd blow up from on my stilts. Every so often one of the farmers' market stand workers would bring their children, and if I kept their kids entertained during the farmers' market I would leave with a case of blueberries or bag full of fruit.

There was a street performer I looked up to named Robert Nelson, who went by the name Butterfly Man. He was short like me and bald right on top of his head, my genetic destiny. Right in the middle of the C-shaped bull's-eye of hair was a tattoo of a beautiful and colorful butterfly.

The butterfly on his head made me think of the caterpillar that butterfly started as. When a caterpillar wraps itself in a chrysalis to become a butterfly, it first must turn into an entirely liquid soup inside of that chrysalis. There has to be nothing left of the caterpillar, only runny liquid. And goo. And mess. And only then it becomes a butterfly.

At that point in my life, I definitely felt like goo. Interactions with the Butterfly Man helped me lock in on my perspective. Before passing his hat, the Butterfly Man always ended with a poem he would recite while four large, flat, perfectly white rings were flying in an arc over his head:

> It matters not
> The job you've got
> As long as you do it well.
> Now the things that are made
> By plans well-laid.
> The test of time will tell.
> But you cannot count
> Or know the amount
> Or the value of a man.
> By the show displayed
> Or the beauty made
> By the touch of the juggler's hand.

There is something fiercely meditative about juggling on the street. I felt like Philippe Petit, the tightrope walker who crossed the Twin Towers in 1974. He was 1,312 feet above the ground for forty-five minutes with no permits or permissions, committing the artistic crime of the century. He and

I were public poetry in motion. Neither he nor I had any specific permissions to be street performing. Often the police would try to shut me down or chase me out of the park. Police at the Pike Place Market were some of the most hostile toward buskers, which was ridiculous as well as unconstitutional because it had been ruled in court that requiring street performers in Seattle to obtain permits or only perform in certain public areas is a violation of the buskers' First Amendment rights.[4] Even when I pointed this out to the police, they chased me out anyway.

This was the only way I'd found to make an income, and it was being taken from me just because the police felt like it. The criminalization of being poor is so entrenched in policing and largely supported by the wealthy society that is Seattle. But I had no other choice, so once they left, I'd get right back to it. Sometimes the police would threaten me with a fine, jail, or, what felt the most personal and hurtful to me, throwing away my juggling supplies. As an autistic person, I was definitely taking my chances with this line of work. Police often find interactions with autistic people more difficult because we do not fit into the box of how they expect people to behave or communicate. They may not know why autistic people rock, or flap their hands, or may get angry at autistic people for not answering questions in the way they expect. Autistic people just see the world differently, and it's a common autistic trait to first respond by asking a question when something doesn't make logical sense.

Can you see how a police officer, used to automatic obedience, could easily interpret this as disrespect? This is why people with disabilities are such frequent targets of police brutality, with between 33 and 50 percent of those who are killed by police being people with disabilities.[5] Furthermore, if you are a disabled Black person, there is a 55 percent chance that you will be arrested by the age of twenty-eight.[6] My friend Haben Girma, a Black deaf-blind Harvard Law graduate, explains this better than I do:

> If you are wondering why disabled people experience higher rates of police violence: Police walk into situations expecting people to hear their spoken commands, see their visual commands, physically be able to move in a certain way to obey physical commands, and other ableist expectations. When disabled people don't respond to commands because we can't, then police use force. There are many stories of family members and friends telling police a person is disabled, but the police don't believe them or don't care. Our current police system is killing disabled people. We need a bold new system to keep our communities safe.

I was lucky that the police only chased me away, when far too many of my disabled peers end up dead after interactions with police. Maybe it was the unicycle and tuxedo or the long, striped stilt pants and balloons. I know my whiteness contributed. At any rate, street performing while disabled was a risky line of work for me. But once again, what choice did I have? I needed to make money. No one would hire me. And the entire country got a minimum wage of $7.25 except for the lucky, segregated, developmentally disabled few for whom our laws say that minimum wage does not apply. But it was okay. Because I loved busking. I loved it. And besides, everyone who saw me smiled, and I was content with this sense that I had taken back some power over my life. Better a witty fool than a foolish wit. I have never gotten to just live my life without being laughed at, talked about, made fun of, mocked, or called weird. When I am performing, at least I am owning this. At least I am taking back control and giving people permission to laugh at me. I shouldn't have to do this for the world to understand and accept me, but I do. As Shakespeare says, "The fool doth think he is wise, but the wise man knows himself to be a fool."

I had been the fool my whole life, but at least now on the street it was by choice and I was being paid to be it.

For three months that year I got a break from street performing out in the elements. I was working at Seattle Children's Theatre, the very theatre that first showed me humanity. It felt like such a full-circle connection with my Geema to be back here, but this time as a performer. I felt such strong personal pride in myself, having worked hard to grow from a nonspeaking child to a performer on that stage. I quietly hoped I would bring the same sense of joy, acceptance, and empowerment to a kid like me who might be in one of my audiences. Unfortunately, my experience was very different as an adult. During the first show I performed at the theatre, I received a phone call from the artistic director on her cell phone during her commute home from work. "I'm driving through a tunnel now so if the call gets dropped I'm going to call you again when I get home, but I wanted you to hear from me as soon as possible," she said more loudly than she needed to, not knowing whether her cell's speaker phone was picking her up or not. She informed me that she had heard from a few actors that much of the chorus was making fun of me. "I wanted to call to apologize on their behalf and let you know that I will not stand for that."

Now, at this point I was an adult in my early twenties. I hadn't realized that people had been making fun of me until I received this phone call. I am always an optimist and always assume that people are trustworthy, doing the best that they can, and working hard to be my friend. In that moment, all my interactions with these friends replayed through my head, and I realized they had been laughing at me, trying to hurt me, not laughing *with* me.

Despite the call from the artistic director, the first two shows I was in at SCT, I was made fun of constantly. Even though I was an audience favorite in the shows, many of the chorus dancers hated me. In musicals, the chorus dancers are all supposed to be nearly identical, flat characters, paper dolls. You have to do all the same dance steps with the goal of each person looking identical to the next. This theatrical idea is so ableist, assuming that all bodies can or should move in an identical way. I didn't know how to reach this nonautistic neutral. I was just a living, breathing person. Most people in the chorus didn't like that there was something different about me and hated others' curiosity or admiration of me. My directors loved that I was different! I remember being in the dance portion of my audition for a musical. Dance auditions are notorious for being incredibly fast paced. Directors and choreographers are looking at not only dance skills, but also how quickly you can learn choreography. They go through the moves with you a couple of times, but quickly the big group following the choreographer becomes groups of five or six with no one to follow.

Sure enough, I got to a point in the choreography where I confidently did a double turn, but upon coming out of the turn so proud that I had successfully landed it, before realizing that all the other dancers were dancing something completely different. I had no idea where I was in the music or the dance anymore, so without missing a beat I just started freestyling, rocking out for the final eight counts, striking a bold pose on the final note, smiling more broadly and genuinely than anyone else. The lone figure in blue jeans and a polo shirt, surrounded by leotards and bike shorts. I was sure I'd blown it but was proud of myself for staying positive, and I encouraged myself that I might get called in to audition again sometime for some other show.

Walking out of the theatre after my audition, I passed by the choreographer. She said she'd be seeing me soon, which I took to mean as I was right and would probably get another shot at auditioning for a different show one day. I was surprised to hear a few weeks later that they were offering me a role! The director and choreographer loved that I had handled the situation with such grace, creativity, and life and wanted that unbridled joy in their production. The show opened, and I was a bit of a left shark before packed houses. The other dancers hit their marks in unison, years of training keeping them all in sharp unity, while my autistic body was just naturally drawn to holding itself in different shapes. But I owned it, just living in every moment, and the audience loved that I was so alive onstage.

The other chorus actors didn't take too kindly to realizing that all their years of training couldn't win them the affection of the audience, and they expressed that by withholding their affection from me. They would change choreography to spite me, doing things like taking a prop that was supposed to be thrown to me for me to catch mid-dance, and instead throw it offstage while whispering, "Fetch" to me. These chorus actors didn't realize that our differences are our strengths and that we are all stronger together. I made the conscious decision to never let this faze me.

During one production I thought I had made true friends. Every time I did something a certain way, said something a certain way, my fully grown adult friends would have me put money into a little box in their dressing room. For a pizza party, they told me. A "Mickey" box. I thought that this was proof of their friendship. I felt so lucky and special that the girls' dressing room had created a little box with my name on it. Why would they have me put my money into a box for a pizza party of all things if they were not friends with me? Pizza parties were something that friends did together, after all. This act of theirs was proof that they were not just my colleagues but also my friends. They had taken time to decorate a box, putting my name on it, almost like a friendship bracelet, I thought.

Sure enough, every time I did something a certain way, or said something a certain way, they would laugh and point at the box, and in my bus money would go. But it was surely a worthwhile investment for this friendship.

It was only one day in the last week of the show when I suggested that we should do the pizza party during our lunch break that they let me know they had already done the pizza party. "We didn't know you thought you would be invited," I remember one larger dark-haired girl telling me while holding back a belly laugh.

I had paid for the entire pizza party because they had insisted that they were my friends. But I suppose for all those months their reality had been different than mine. This felt worse than being ignored.

As I walked home that night, the cold Seattle raindrops pattered hypnotically against the side of my head, down the back of my neck. Like a stim, they drowned out all the unwanted. I kept my headphones pressed tight over my ears, though I'm still not sure what I was trying to shut out.

When someone is cruel, mean, unkind, bad, or a bully, it has nothing to do with you and everything to do with them. When you choose not to allow their behavior to affect you, you take all their power away from them. I just did my best every day and was kind every day to everyone. I did my job while ignoring all the extra baggage. I quickly learned not to let these people affect me. Their behavior was a statement about them, not me.

Even outside of the theatre, I was often made fun of because socializing didn't come intuitively or naturally to me. When you aren't being social, it sometimes misleads people into thinking that you don't want to be friends with them. People thought I stood back and didn't chat with them because I didn't want to be their friend, but that couldn't have been further from the truth. I just didn't instinctively know how to make a friend. Being autistic sometimes feels like everyone else can communicate telepathically, while I'm solely reliant on them saying exactly what they actually mean. Social skills and social norms are difficult for autistic people to pick up on, although we notice everyone else seeming to have no trouble being on the same page with each other. If you see an autistic person standing by themselves, you can invite them into your circle of friends. Know that even if they don't actively participate or speak much, they might be thrilled just to get to be listening and included just standing with you. Or they might say that they want alone time, and that is okay too! It doesn't mean they don't like you or don't want to be your friend.

I always showed up early to places, just as a way to get comfortable in my surroundings before more people arrived and made it uncomfortable again. I was once told by a stage manager not to be "creepy" in regard to my showing up an hour or two early to the theatre. I never bothered anyone, just sat with my headphones on listening to a book on tape. But to nonautistic people this is "creepy." I sometimes wonder how some people can be so preoccupied with what autistic people are doing, especially when so often we are making a point to not be intrusive or a bother—and yet, somehow this is exactly what makes us stand out. It's an impossible game to win.

I ultimately performed in eight productions at Seattle Children's Theatre in the whole decade of my twenties, but I never once had a speaking role. No matter how happy hearted I was while working at that theatre, even though the company loved me and hired me again and again, I was frequently made fun of, intentionally excluded, and alienated by the other actors. Working at SCT should have been a dream come true, but my autism had gotten in the way.

This was around that same time that I officially received my diagnosis. I always knew I was different before this, and I knew I was treated differently than most people. I had heard people's voices raise when they spoke to me the way someone might raise their voice talking to a toddler. I knew that I was different enough to need to go to special education. But no adult had ever specifically told me why or how I was different. So, upon graduating from college I had been seeing a therapist to help me process my struggles building connections with other people. As I described to them my difficulty intuiting social norms, my uncertainty about how to make a friend, and my sensory processing issues, they suspected that I might be autistic and decided that I should be referred to an autism specialist.

Now, despite their professional opinion, a general therapist is not allowed to or qualified to diagnose autism. You need a specialist. However, most autism centers only diagnose people under the age of eighteen. At the time of writing this, the CDC admits that there is no psychometrically validated test for diagnosing adults with autism. It is very difficult to find a specialist in something that doesn't have an established procedure for diagnosis. America is so determined to erase the existence of autistic adults that it doesn't even have an official, standardized test with which to use as a tool in diagnosing autism in adults. Perhaps this is why I often find that when nonautistic people picture an autistic person in their head, they nearly always picture a child. But again, autistic children grow up into autistic adults. And usually when they do, they disappear into unemployment and segregation.

Fortunately for me, Seattle actually does have an adult autism clinic, and I finally ended up with a referral to the University of Washington's Adult Autism Clinic. These appointments book out many, many months in advance for new patients. Once I finally received my appointment, though, the meeting was only a few *hours* long, which is extremely quick compared to the process for diagnosing a child. The room was much like any other therapist's room I'd been in before: a very fashionably curated living room that is also trying *very hard* to be casual and welcoming.

Therapists of old may have had you lie down on a couch in order to relax, but apparently today's therapists try to get you to let your guard down with creature comforts like textured throw blankets and bowls of Skittles. Dr. Freed engaged me in open dialogue but checked off boxes from one of the tests that is used to diagnose children as we spoke. I preferred this kind of testing interaction to a sterile Q and A interrogation. She tilted her head and listened carefully to what I said, sometimes sharing observations such as that I seemed to display signs of social anxiety. Eventually I left with "Autism Spectrum Disorder" written on a piece of paper. This was the first time I had heard those words directly in connection with myself. I felt a huge sense of relief! Much like when six-year-old Mickey first tried on his red glasses and could finally see multiple parts of a tree, the diagnosis was a lens that finally brought my whole confusing life into focus. My whole life I had known I was different. I was treated differently, people spoke to me differently, I went to school differently. I was not surprised by this diagnosis, but I was very relieved. Blood rushed back out of my cheeks, which felt like they had been flushed my whole life, moving back down through my chest, off my shoulders, traveling clearly now through the rest of my body.

When you've felt so different your whole life, it is truly such a weight lifted when you know that there is an explanation. Suddenly you are no longer adrift on a lonely sea, but you are anchored by a name for the thing, and then you find safe harbor in the knowledge that there's a community of other people who feel and think the same way you do and are going through the same things you are. There were other people who experienced the world the same way I did! People who thought the way I did! I wasn't stupid, or bad, or weird. There was a name for it.

Although I was now equipped and feeling empowered by a diagnosis, auditioning was a struggle. Outside of nonspeaking roles at Seattle Children's Theatre and Seattle Opera, I was not getting cast. This had everything to do with disability, in particular my blindness. I am low vision, which means I see the world through a Vaseline-like filter, even if I'm wearing my glasses or contacts. I have extremely limited peripheral vision, and I do not have a driver's license. I can only read large-print text for short periods of time before my eyes lose their ability to focus and read the words at all, and I have to look away from the page for a time and try to reset. Writing this book has so far included lots of voice-to-text writing, with others helping me go through after the fact and edit the voice-to-text typos. I often wander around my neighborhood dictating sentences into my phone. Unfortunately for me, the traditional American theatre audition process is inherently inaccessible to people with vision impairment.

Knowing whether to out yourself as disabled at an audition or job interview is always a struggle. If you tell the world you are disabled, you will be discriminated against. Disability is still the one holdout where people think it is not only right but obvious that your disability status would be a deciding factor at a job interview. This is evidenced by the fact that even though it is illegal to discriminate against someone solely because they have a disability, it is also very legal to not pay them a minimum wage solely because of their disability. Every other protected class in America gets a minimum wage, but if you are disabled you are supposed to simply be grateful that an employer even gave you a job to do for pennies an hour.

If, however, you don't tell the world you are disabled, then you don't get the things that you need. We live in a society designed for and by non-disabled people. Inaccessibility is the design standard, and accessibility is almost always no more than a tacked-on afterthought, if it's even considered at all. Think about your home, or the homes of all your friends. Are any of them wheelchair accessible? Or are most homes in this country built with the assumption that you won't ever be socializing with someone who uses a wheelchair? Small print is the standard text size things are printed in, even though if large print were the standard, more people would be able to read easily. Legally blind folx aside, how many elderly people in your life find small print difficult to read? As a disability rights advocate in my thirties, I now advocate for universal design: design that has accessibility to all built into it. This includes things like ramps in an airport, which not only make a space accessible for those who use mobility devices but also make life easier for business travelers rolling their luggage, and mothers and fathers pushing strollers. It also includes having captions on videos, which not only allows d/Deaf and hard-of-hearing folx to watch the video, but it also allows people to watch the video while in the library, in a waiting room, or on public transportation. Universal design helps us all, not just those of us with disabilities. But in this country, inaccessibility is the primary design standard. If you need an accommodation due to disability, you have to ask for it and hope that the person in power decides to give it to you.

For me, universal design is also about the need to get the text of my scripts enlarged. Otherwise, I've been in a lot of messes of auditions where the audition wasn't really about my acting or storytelling, or connecting with my scene partner, changing and being changed by them. The auditions were just a vision test where the director took the role of the doctor, handing me the script, and saying, "Can you read this eleven-point font?" "Can you read the bottom line on this eye chart?" And you spend the ten minutes working out what that eye chart says instead of acting or showing them how you could collaborate together on a show. If I can somehow get through the audition fiasco and get cast, I'm at a point then where I can make the necessary accommodations for myself. When I'm cast in a show, I secretly record the first readthrough of the show on my phone. (I have to do this secretly due to the actors' union rules that prohibit recordings.) Much like the assumptions built into inaccessible houses, the union makes these rules assuming that someone with vision difficulties would never be working at that caliber of theatre. But if I break the rule in secret with my phone hidden in my pocket, then I can take my eyes out of the equation and simply memorize my lines by listening to the recording. I'd rather not have to break rules, but I have found that if you try to play by the rules in a game designed to make disabled folx lose, you won't ever win. I know because I have tried following the rule book.

When I secured an audition slot, I would often ask whether they could have large-print sides available for me on the day of the audition. Sides are the pages of script that they have you read in an audition. No one has time to see you act out the whole show in an audition, nor is it necessary for a director to consider that much material in order to be able to assess you for the part. Usually just a page or three of the script suffices, and they usually print several copies of them out and have them available for actors to read from at the audition. So, I would ask if they could just make one copy of those pages in large print for me. Only on three occasions out of hundreds of auditions did I actually receive these large-print sides. Most of the time, regardless of the number of emails I sent, auditors would just "forget" to enlarge my audition scripts. Disabled people learn out of necessity to be innovative problem solvers to get by in a world ruled by nondisabled people, and I came up with another easy option for them to level the playing field for me. I'd say that if they *couldn't* print the sides in large print, that was just fine, but could they send the sides to me a few days in advance of the audition so that I could enlarge my own scripts? But many theatre companies refused, stating that this would be giving me an unfair advantage over the nondisabled actors. Neither one of these options, printing one copy in a larger font or sending me the sides in advance, would have been a significant burden of work for these theatre companies. Despite this, they still refused to make these accommodations.

Theatre companies might not ever come out and openly admit that they don't want to work with people with disabilities, but they make it abundantly clear by their firm refusal to make reasonable accommodations. (And people say that autistics lack empathy.) Theatres claim that they don't want to give me an unfair advantage, but are they really unable to see that nondisabled actors already have every advantage over disabled actors, in both the theatre industry and society at large? Do they really not see that they are not giving me an advantage, but rather they are leveling the playing field by simply offering me scripts I can read? (And apparently, I'm the one who's blind.) But of course, I doubt they are actually unable to see this, but simply unwilling. Ableism is one of the frameworks this society is built on, and people cling desperately to its familiarity, even though it oppresses 20 percent of the population.[7] Yes, the oppression of disabled people is familiar to society. To so many people, that's just how the world works.

So, I stopped asking for these enlargements. Society told me that the reasonable accommodation I needed, made legal by the Americans with Disabilities Act, was too much to ask for. Even though the ADA enshrines in law that it is unethical to not make reasonable accommodation for disabled folx, theatre companies would try to gaslight me into believing that I was the unethical one asking for an unfair advantage. So, I stopped. What was I going to do? Try to sue a theatre for not providing me large-print sides? And then what? Never work in theatre again. Always be seen as the actor who made trouble and tried to bankrupt a theatre. No. I had no choice. I stopped asking for what I needed. I started to believe people who told me that it wasn't my eyesight making it difficult for me to read small-print scripts. It was just that I wasn't a talented actor.

I think that there's a false dichotomy right now where people say that the most talented person should get the part. Even if the most talented person should theoretically get the part, or the job, or the position, we're not doing a very good job right now of assessing who's talented, or even what talent means, when you're asking an actor to read text that is far too small for him to read instead of seeing how well that actor can act and connect to a scene partner with appropriately sized text. Our job as storytellers is to help people see themselves. And help people see life experiences very different from their own. What we are doing isn't as linear as running a race or climbing a mountain. Our job as actors is just to be a living, breathing person. And disability doesn't make you any less of a living, breathing person. I'd hope that one day, there could be an autistic person playing Hamlet, or playing King Lear and that the story wouldn't be about autism. The character would just be a person who happens to be autistic and who also happens to be the Prince of Denmark or an aging king, and that there wouldn't be too many questions about it. But until we get there, in the meantime, it would be really nice if when we see an amputee in a movie, the character was actually played by an amputee, that someone was given that opportunity to shine at least then if there are not other roles they would be given the opportunity to shine in.

For a producer, I know it is easier and more affordable for an amputee to wear a prosthetic and long pants in order to play a nondisabled character than it is to digitally remove a nondisabled actor's legs in postproduction to have them play an amputee. Yet productions always choose the latter. God forbid they hire a disabled person! When we see a character with a disability onstage, I'd love to see people representing their own community accurately, the way that community would hope to be represented. More than nice—it would be right. But that is not the world we live in, and I continued only playing nonspeaking roles at theatres that already personally knew and liked me.

Being resilient is one of my strengths, so despite rejection after gaslit rejection, I kept at the auditioning game. One day I was auditioning for a play at ACT Theatre in Seattle. I don't think the casting director knew I was autistic, but she must have been able to just intuit that I was. Many people can just tell. She handed me a book that she had prepared by highlighting a monologue within it. "Mickey," she said, "I have just gotten back from seeing this play at the National Theatre in London. There is no way we will be able to do this play at ACT anytime soon because it is going to go on to Broadway after its run at the National. But you need to read it. It is based on this book. This character is you."

I looked at the book she had handed me and read. I slowly sounded out the small-print words: "The . . . Curioouuus Incident of . . . the Dog . . . in the . . . Night-Time." I gave that audition my best stab, cold reading the small print. But it captured my attention, and I knew I had to go home and dedicate some time to finding an accessible version of the text for me to dive into. Christopher, the main character in this monologue, was autistic.

Later that night I found the audiobook version and immersed myself into the world of Christopher and his adventures through the London subways to find his mother and solve a crime against a neighbor's dog. Representation matters. Much like when I received my autism diagnosis, *The Curious Incident of the Dog in the Night-Time* made me realize there really are other people like me out there in the world. It reminded me that I am not weird, or stupid, or bad, but just like Christopher I am powerful, and I can do whatever I want to do and accomplish the goals I want to accomplish. I read the book and knew I was not alone. I had a community. I had a people. I also knew that I needed to play this part. The show was going to be on Broadway next, in New York City. I lived in Seattle. I didn't have an agent. But I did have three things: courage, imagination, and determination.

6

She is a metal pole in zero-degree weather; I'm afraid if I touch my tongue to her it will stick forever.

—Unknown

I was twenty-one when I had my first girlfriend, first kiss, and first experience of sex. Anika and I had vaguely known each other for a few years beforehand. We had gone to the same high school but were in different grades. A few years later I was a sophomore in college, and she was a senior in high school, but we'd somehow kept in touch enough to find ourselves chatting over Facebook Messenger one night.

Sometimes autistic people find online communication more comfortable than in-person interaction. You have a little bit more time to plan out what you're going to say, and you only have to worry about what's being communicated through typing, instead of also interpreting body language. I was confessing to her that I was going to have to kiss someone in a play for college, and I was feeling nervous because I hadn't kissed anyone in real life yet and didn't know what to do! I was very surprised when Anika promptly offered to be my first kiss. I of course decided to take her up on the offer. We made plans to meet up at the Seattle Center, underneath the Space Needle, by a choreographed musical fountain that children run though and the elderly, housing-insecure hippies who live at Seattle Center dance in. The thing happened and it was . . . fine. Lips touched lips. If there was supposed to be some cosmic spark in the moment, there wasn't. But I was most relieved to know it wasn't so hard, and that it would go just fine when it was time to rehearse the college play.

I was also excited to have experienced a new kind of closeness to a girl. I'd spent the past few years feeling attracted to girls, but figuring out how to act on this impulse and curiosity was a new puzzle. Just like making friends wasn't intuitive for me, neither was expressing romantic attraction.

I was once told in college that to let someone know you were attracted to them, you should look at them, and not look away. For me, this tactic of staring did not yield the desired results. If a handsome man stared at a woman, there would be "come hither" embers burning beneath his eyes. His face would be relaxed and approachable with just the faintest hint of a smile in the corners of his mouth. He would continue talking nonchalantly with his many friends as he made eyes with the woman as if the burning chemistry between them was just incidental and not planned, rehearsed, constructed. It would all be very nonchalant. Nonchalant is a word whose meaning I understand intellectually yet have no concept of how to conjure into any type of reality.

If I stare at a woman, it looks as though I am lost, asking silently yet desperately for help, and the woman is left feeling confused, concerned, and worst of all, uncomfortable. Sometimes, usually, I see a kind pity in their eyes. It's like everyone else has a key to this thing and I just misplaced mine somewhere.

Maybe, I thought, *if I could just master some sort of a geek chic look.* But I'm always told that my smile is just too big. That I am trying just too hard.

It also didn't help that healthy romantic affection had never been modeled for me at home. I'd never once seen my mom and dad kiss on the lips. I'd only seen my dad come up behind my mom every once in a while and kiss her on the ear, to which she would briskly snap, "What are you doing?"

But here was a girl who initiated a romantic connection with me, and I wanted to make the most of my shot at this. We kept spending time together, and about a month later we decided to officially become boyfriend and girlfriend. The birds were flying high and knew exactly how I felt! It was a new dawn, it was a new day, it was a new life for me, and to quote the great Nina Simone, I was feeling pretty darn good! I had done it! I had someone to care about and call my own, someone who was delighted to tell the world that she liked me. More than anything, I felt lucky to *finally* have a friend.

I had so many moments of adventure and new experiences, all sprinkled throughout my days with a girl by my side. That year we smoked pot together twice, and then she burned my eyebrow with the lighter, so we never did it again.

Anika was a little bit of a new age hippie, unbound by what was "cool" or in. She was always drinking hot tea with a loud slurp, explaining to me that this was the only proper way to sip tea. Every text message Anika sent me was like a miniature poem.

Never: "Hang out after class tonight?"

Instead:

> It's dark.
> I stumble and fall into your eyes,
> their doors wide open.
> I am drowning in blue happiness.
> It's dark.
> Am I lost?
> I wander the night terrain
> following the black north star,
> your pupil
> through knees and elbows and sheets.

What a text message! I felt like her cellular muse every time I received a text message from her.

Her Nordic hair was full of tight-knotted gold curls, and she smelled like that kind of summer sweet that sometimes happens when you sleep well but get a little sweaty. Her lips tasted of that same sleepy sweetness.

We made love on a dock at Luther Burbank Park, as well as at the shore club. We made love over the water, under the stars, in broad daylight hiding in the park, and we snuck her in after Gee and Gramps were asleep to make love in that house too. When our antics attracted the attention and disapproval of our respective adults, she and I weren't allowed to see each other. Undeterred, we snuck out every night to go on adventures together. We adventured from midnight until 3:00 a.m. for over five months until we realized that sleep was not a luxury. We found out that the code to the alarm at her house was 1991, but then her mom read her diary entry about us sitting all night on the neighbors' roof, and then the code changed to 1954.

Having a girlfriend was all fun and games until her senior year came to an end and she went away to college. "University of Portland," she told me one day as we were sitting on our usual dock over the lake slurping tea in the only acceptable way.

"It's a Catholic school . . . ," she said midsigh, "But it's Portland! So"—her enthusiasm peaking on the word "Portland," which has the city motto "Keep Portland Weird"—"you can take the BoltBus and we can still be hippie friends."

"What's a hippie friend?" I asked, half hoping it was just another word for girlfriend and boyfriend.

"A friend who you can kiss," she said. And I never saw her again.

That was the end of that. I was alone again. It was a bit sad to see such a magical chapter close, but not heartbreaking, I guess. It had been great to finally have a close friend, and it was great to finally be having sex and kissing, but at no point did I love her. It was an enjoyable experience for both of us at that moment in each of our lives, but never was there any sense of cosmic spark or deep, lasting connection. When it ended, there was not much to grieve; I suppose more than anything we were friends: first friends. And I was relieved to know that making a friend who wanted to go on adventures with me was something I could do. It rocketed my confidence like nothing else.

After that, working in the theatre industry as well as online dating brought some women my way every now and then. I found that people only ever wanted to be friends with benefits with me. They very much enjoyed adventurous, unbridled sex with a sensory-seeking autistic person who wasn't a slave to social norms. Partners loved that I could openly and unapologetically talk about sex and sexuality in a straightforward way. For once my complete lack of a verbal filter paid off! By no verbal filter, I mean that I merely say precisely what I think. In some situations that kind of directness can make people feel that you are weird or even rude. But in the bedroom, people sometimes think that it is astoundingly sexy. Partners also loved that I was sensory seeking. What is foreplay after all if not simply sensory play? Is there anything autistic people are more expert at than sensory play? I think not. The tingle of nails gently running up a spine, or a slight tug on an earlobe or the bristling hair at the base of a neck. Sometimes sensory play is a kiss in just the right spot behind someone's ear where their hairline meets their neck. This is where sensory-seeking autistic people excel! Disability is sexy! Differences are sexy! You think I'm sexy, right? Disability is sexy, and I'm not afraid to say it!

Yet, for my partners, publicly and exclusively committing to me was apparently not so sexy. It was disappointing but not necessarily surprising.

I felt ashamed that even people who liked being intimate with me were humiliated to publicly admit it. Warmth flooded my flushed cheeks every time I was told why my relationship with a partner must remain secret.

When you are disabled, you are told your whole life that you should just feel lucky if *anyone* is interested in you romantically. My own grandfather had counseled me to that effect: "Boy, Mick, you'll sure be lucky to find someone who wants to be your wife. That will have to be quite the unique person"—his voice strained while spinning strings of cheese around his fork. Strangers had made comments to that effect too, as I was packing up my stilts and balloons after long days of street performing. I just figured I'd better take what I could get in that arena and not be too picky. I had no real expectation that I'd ever actually get cast as the male romantic lead in some grand, epic love story, whether in real life or onstage. Eventually I met someone online who very quickly expressed interest in a relationship with me and then soon after expressed interest in marriage. So, I ended up ignoring a multitude of red flags and getting married to the first person who wanted to marry me, with two kids arriving soon after. No breaking news headlines: "BREAKING: Autistic person finds partner." No ticker-tape parade. But here I was.

7

Play a mental, win an Oscar.

—Kate Winslet, playing herself on the TV show *Extras*

To get cast in *Curious Incident* I had one major problem. It was a disabled role, and I was a disabled actor. Let me just lay out for you how big this big problem was. Buckle up, friends.

There is a joke in Hollywood that the surest way to win an Oscar is to have a nondisabled actor play a disabled role. Unfortunately, this isn't only a joke but also a fact, and all the Hollywood executives are well aware. They know it is not right too. Disability rights groups meet with top executives every year and each time say that it isn't right. But if you are a nondisabled actor playing a disabled role who receives a nomination, you have a nearly 50 percent chance of winning an Oscar.[1] In fact, since 1989, 50 percent of actors who won the Oscar for Best Actor won for being nondisabled actors who played disabled roles.[2] Imagine if 50 percent of actors who won the Oscar for Best Actor in recent years had won for being white actors pretending to be Black or Asian. People wouldn't stand for it. To put this in perspective, this year for the very first time in its ninety-three-year history, the Oscars nominated a person with a visible disability. For the first time ever. Only one nominee. Nominated for the category of Best Documentary.[3] But having nondisabled actors in cripface wins awards, earns critical acclaim, and makes money, so Hollywood is more than happy to tune out the disability community and let it continue.

We know from the census that 20 percent of the American population has a disability. One out of every five people. Yet less than 1 percent of the characters we see on TV have disabilities. Of that small 1 percent of disabled characters, 95 percent of those are played by nondisabled actors.

I'm gonna say it again for the people in the back: 95 percent of disabled characters are played by nondisabled actors!

All of these statistics mean that for the 20 percent of the population that has a disability, there are less than 0.05 percent of roles being cast with disabled actors.[4] And I thought TV and movies' jobs were to present our country and our world as it is at its fullest. But disability has again been made to disappear, slipping away through the cracks.

Broadway is much the same. *But me getting cast in* Curious Incident *could help turn that tide,* I thought to myself!

Think about how horrible it feels for a disabled person to watch some nondisabled actor bring to life all of their ill-informed, ignorant ideas and stereotypes about how a disabled person acts, moves, speaks, and thinks, often for laughs, and then see them be awarded for bringing their stereotypes to life. Meanwhile disabled people are not even allowed to play ourselves onstage or on-screen. If you do not have lived experience, all you have are assumptions, and it really hurts to see someone play out stereotypical or even bold assumptions onstage or in a movie.

Why are audiences so enthralled by watching countless cripfaced performances? I really like the way disabled playwright Christopher Shinn paraphrases the late, disabled playwright John Belluso's theory on why actors who play disabled characters often win Oscars: "It is reassuring for the audience to see an actor like Daniel Day Lewis, after so convincingly portraying disability in My Left Foot, get up from his seat in the auditorium and walk to the stage to accept his award. There is a collective 'Phew' as people see it was all an illusion. Society's fear and loathing around disability, it seems, can be magically transcended."

Nondisabled members of society have been socialized to feel incredibly uncomfortable around disability. It starts when children, with all their beautiful, curious, innocent wonder at all things in the world, look inquisitively toward someone with a visible disability, and their adults take this wonderful learning opportunity and squander it on a brief admonishment that it's rude to stare. The silent implication is that they should just pretend that the disabled person doesn't exist. If the child asks a disabled person a question about their disability, the child is quickly scolded by their caregiver for being so rude. Those children grow into adults who can't bear to think about, talk about, or acknowledge disability. People aren't even comfortable saying the word "disabled," instead choosing to say "special needs," "handicapable," or "differently abled." They feel uncomfortable seeing a disabled character accurately portrayed by a disabled actor because they've always been taught that it's socially unacceptable to look at disabled people. They much prefer having a nondisabled actor play the role, so that when the nondisabled audience feels pity, disgust, or any other uncomfortable feeling while having to look at disability, this discomfort is instantly relieved when they see the nondisabled actor effortlessly shed the disability to receive the award or take the bow.

Erasing community groups from media representation or news coverage is what happens when society wishes they could erase that community group from real life. I believe that even if they wouldn't say it outright, society wishes that disabled people would just disappear. Nonintegrated special education acts as segregation between disabled and nondisabled students, with the disabled kids ushered away into a different classroom hidden in the back of the school. Special ed goes away once they graduate from high school, so they are again segregated into unemployment. It's why when a parent of a disabled child murders that child, the media is overwhelmingly supportive of the parent. It's why disabled characters make up less than 1 percent of the characters we see represented in entertainment, and why nondisabled people are hired to play 95 percent of that 1 percent of disabled roles. It's why up to 50 percent of people murdered by police are disabled. It's why an estimated 67 percent of pregnancies that receive a prenatal diagnosis of Down syndrome are terminated.[5] Society is already doing plenty to erase the existence of disabled people. But going so far as to not even say the word "disabled"? *Now y'all just seem petty.*

Now, I don't think that most nondisabled people genuinely wish death upon disabled people. But I do think that they have been socialized to feel intensely uncomfortable around disability, and in this hyperconvenient, self-serving society, we rid ourselves of anything inconvenient or uncomfortable. People are so keen to erase disability, but in doing so they erase the people with disabilities. They erase me. In the disability community there is a big push to get people comfortable saying the word "disability," so as to not erase disability. People often use words like "special needs" to describe people with developmental disabilities such as autism or Down syndrome. But special would be if I always needed to eat dinosaur eggs for breakfast. Special would be if I always needed to sleep in a tree house or a rocket ship. I need employment, I need love and support and acceptance, and I need to be invited to the diversity and inclusion table. Those are human needs. There isn't anything special about them.

People so badly want to make us disabled folx disappear or go away. Even when people want to read or watch stories about disability like *Wonder* or *Me before You*, they so badly don't want any actually disabled people involved in the making of those stories. That's why both those books were written by nondisabled writers who did little to no research into the disability community. That's why both of the movies made from these books had nondisabled actors cast in the leading disabled roles and why both movies were written and directed by nondisabled people who also did little to no research into the disability community. But here's the thing: not all representation is good representation. Not only do we need disabled actors cast in disabled roles, and books like *Wonder* and *Me before You* that are solely about disability to be written by disabled authors or with the help of the disability community, but we also need these roles to exist free from problematic narratives about disability.

The stories we tell matter. The characters in those stories matter. Representation matters. Good representation matters.

It may not surprise you to know that the book *Curious Incident* is often used to train both police and firefighters about autism. What *might* surprise you is that Mark Haddon, the author of *Curious Incident*, who states he is not autistic, said this on his website:

> Unsurprisingly, I'm often asked to talk about Asperger's and autism or to become involved with organizations who work on behalf of people with Asperger's and autism, many of whom do wonderful work. but I always decline, for two reasons. I know very little about the subject. I did no research for 'Curious incident' (other than photographing the interiors of Swindon and Paddington stations). Imagination always trumps research. I thought that if I could make Christopher real to me then he'd be real to readers. Judging by the reaction, it seems to have worked. [. . .] To become a spokesperson for those with Asperger's or autism, or to present myself as some kind of expert in the field, would completely undermine this, and make me look like a fool into the bargain.[6]

Not surprisingly, in this book written by a nonautistic author who did not research autism, there are plenty of things about Christopher that are inaccurate representations of what it is actually like to be autistic.

Yet now *Curious Incident* is one of the primary ways that schoolchildren, police departments, fire departments, physicians, and the public learn about autism! Don't we deserve better? Don't we deserve a little bit of research? Or better yet, don't we deserve to hear directly from the community we want to learn about? I think so. Following the motto of the autistic community "Nothing about us without us."

With 33 to 50 percent of people who are killed by police being disabled, it is crucial that police have access to materials about autism that are true and accurate. This is just one example of how inaccurate representation is literally dangerous and harmful to disabled folx.

The media loves to otherize people with disabilities. The play *Curious Incident* was written with one goal in mind: to win awards. It was brilliantly written to achieve that goal. But all that brilliant writing goes into vividly describing just how vastly different the writer believes Christopher to be from everyone else, thus othering him. Othering a person or a group of people is unhelpful because it draws attention to an island without building a bridge between it and the mainland. People are scared to build a bridge to the island, because othering tells them that the island is too far, and the water too rough, and even if you made it over there, the island has strange, scary inhabitants that you must not look at. Othering creates a perception of so little common ground, and so much that is starkly different. But authentic representation is important because it's a lot harder to other someone if they are sitting in the room next to you.

Authenticity is powerful. Authenticity is sexy. You can capture so much more brilliant, honest, three-dimensional nuance with authenticity.

Because of this, I knew I had to get cast in *Curious Incident*. Furthermore, I knew I had to be cast in *Curious Incident* because when we cast actors with disabilities or allow people with disabilities to write books, it has a positive effect that spreads far beyond the entertainment industry. When we cast inclusively, all the business leaders in different fields of work all across the country who see that show or read that book get to see that you can hire people with disabilities. It shows them that people with disabilities can do professional work at the highest level, and that, to quote the musical *Hamilton*—"We get the job done." It demonstrates that employers have no reason to discriminate against people with disabilities, and beyond that they have so many reasons to value hiring disabled people.

People with disabilities are some of the best creative problem solvers in the world. We have to be because every day we navigate a world that was designed nearly exclusively with nondisabled people in mind. With autism comes a new way of thinking; a fresh eye, a fresh mind, literally a completely different wiring of the brain. We are capable of imagining and creating a new world. Can you think of a better creative problem-solving challenge than imagining a new world? A more human and moral world. A kinder world that works for everyone, not just the few. Whether you are autistic or not, thank God for the things that make you different. These are what will help you innovate. Your weaknesses are what make you tenacious in the pursuit of your dreams. Your challenges, the things about yourself you loathe, are what have been training you your whole life to handle this type of problem solving with grace. How lucky the world is for the things that make you different.

While trying to figure out how to get cast, I think about young people with disabilities in this country who need to see positive role models who will tell them that if you are different, if you access the world differently, if you need special accommodations, then the world needs you! Disability is an interesting minority group in that it isn't always genetic. Oftentimes disabled people are the only disabled person in their family. They might not know any other disabled people at all, let alone others with their same disability. But if they can turn on the TV, open a book, or attend a show and see authentically portrayed disabled people, their world becomes much less lonely. The point of storytelling is to connect us with people we otherwise wouldn't come in contact with, to bring us life experiences we don't already have. That is why diversity matters.

Inclusion in art matters because it leads directly to inclusion in life. Unfortunately, this is not accomplished when people with disabilities are even excluded from stories that are entirely about disability, and when those stories are inherently problematic. Disabled kids deserve to see better stories than *Wonder*, where a kid is relentlessly bullied due to his disability, or *Me before You*, where a disabled person kills themself so as not to be a burden. That's nothing new to them and doesn't benefit their lives in any way. Personal aside to you reading this, disabled or not: You are not a burden. Anyone who says otherwise is afraid of your power. You killing yourself so as not to burden others is not a heroic, romantic act and not necessary. We deserve better representation. Representation allows young people to imagine what can be and to be unburdened by what has been. Period.

I'm sure you can think of so many books that revolve around disability, but how many of those books were written from within the disability community?

Young people deserve to see disabled kids excelling and being the heroes of their own stories. I promise you this is also helpful content for nondisabled kids too. Nondisabled kids don't need their only experiences with disability to be damaging tropes. Nobody benefits from this in any real way. Sure, there are awards won and money earned, but at a disproportionately high cost to the 20 percent of the population who identify as disabled. The math just doesn't add up to an overall positive gain for society.

Here is a challenge. Make this book more popular than *Wonder* or *Me before You*, which were both written by nondisabled people with little research put into the actual disability community and then turned into movies written by, directed by, and starring nondisabled people. No need to cancel those stories, but instead uplift this one! You can do it! I believe in you! Tell a friend! Go team!

Can you tell I was passionate about figuring out how to get myself cast in *Curious Incident* even though I lived in Seattle with no agent, no manager, and no travel experience?

For any readers who are in the business of casting and have a growing sense of "but how?!" My advice to you is this: Don't get caught up in the details. Don't let it become a daunting task that paralyzes you. If you are doing the play *The Curious Incident of the Dog in the Night-Time* and can't find an autistic actor to play the role, cast a different large character in the show with an autistic actor, or cast Christopher as someone with a different disability, or as a female disabled actor, or a person of color, and then you are still doing a service to the autism community because so many people truly believe that autistic people always look the same way. In every TV show or movie—think *Atypical*, *The Good Doctor*, dating back to *Rain Man*—autistic people are always white men. And this leads to a major underdiagnosis of women and people of color, affecting who even gets diagnosed with autism, since we know you don't start out by going to a specialist; you start out with a pediatrician or general care practitioner, who likely only studied autism briefly, if at all, during medical school. Then they refer you to the specialist if you check their "A-dar" boxes. And since the pediatrician and general practitioners aren't specialists in autism but *are* going to the theatre, going to the movies, reading books, and watching TV just like everyone else, the place that these people are getting the bulk of their education about what autism looks like is movies, TV shows, and theatre, such as *Atypical*, *The Good Doctor*, and *Rain Man*.

That said, this is certainly not your excuse to not actively find disabled people to hire if you are doing work about disability. Disability is still not thought of when we talk about diversity, and that needs to change. We don't just want to be audience members. We want to be employed. We want to be *active* parts of the conversation *about autism*. We want to help shape the stories about us from the inside just like any other minority group would want to have a hand in telling the public stories that shape public understanding about their group. That is not a right that we have thus far been allowed.

Which brings the story back to me believing that I should be cast in the role of Christopher in *Curious Incident*, despite the fact that the role had never before been played by an autistic actor. I knew that this could change. I knew that my community could represent itself. I knew we could speak for ourselves. In the very last line of the Broadway play, Christopher says, "Does this mean I can do anything?" The world has always told both him and me and people who are different in any way that we cannot. We are told that we can't even tell our own stories. But I believe that if people think you can't do something, it is just a sign of their own lack of creativity and has nothing to do with you. I spent two years trying to educate the industry about this to no avail. I was told that diversity and inclusion only applied to race, gender, and sexuality, but that if I brought up disability I was sorely mistaken about the meaning of diversity. I was told that neurodiversity and disability were not types of diversity, but just things that were wrong with people that needed to be cured, fixed, done away with, or erased. Despite this, I was not deterred. I had a mission. It was an important mission. I knew I could do it. Flip the script. Change the narrative. Get cast in a Broadway show from Seattle with no agent and use that platform to give people like myself a voice. I knew in that moment, "If not me, who? If not now, when?" Get cast in *Curious Incident*. Rant over. My adventure began.

8

It always seems impossible until it's done.

—Nelson Mandela

Society has always told me all the things that I can't. I can't have friends. I can't have a job. I can't marry the woman of my dreams. I am told that I am less. Less smart. Less articulate. Bad. Stupid. I've gotten used to ignoring the voice of society and doing all the things anyway.

When I started raising awareness about the fact that Christopher in *Curious Incident* was always cast with nonautistic actors and stating that an autistic actor should be cast in the role instead, I was told that it wasn't possible because an autistic actor simply wouldn't be capable of playing that role. Never mind that it had never even been attempted before; the theatre industry had already made up its mind on the matter. It was decided and decreed: an autistic actor is incapable of playing such a demanding role, I was foolish to think that I might be an exception to this rule, I should stop striving for it, and I should shut up and sit down.

Now, I'm all too familiar with ignoring society when it tells me what I can't do. That was a nonissue. However, there were some other barriers between me and my goal, and they were both unfamiliar and formidable.

Usually, in order to get cast in a Broadway show, you first need to be living in New York City. You either grow up there, or you move there from somewhere else. It's a notoriously expensive city to live in, so to move there you need to be in possession of a sizable chunk of money that you can risk completely losing in a gamble on a dream. For that, you either need to have come from a wealthy family that is happy to sponsor your dreams, or you need to hustle to hoard money for the big move. You also have to be untethered and free to move. This means that unless you chose early in your career to forgo having a spouse and kids, you either need to have a family that is willing to live without you for however long, or have them be willing to uproot their entire lives to follow your dream. These are just some of the initial barriers.

Once you get to New York, you will likely need an agent. An agent's job is to be your personal representative in the industry. They find auditions to send you on, they pitch you for roles, they help negotiate contracts, and they are the keepers of the contact information of decision-makers in the industry. If you can get an experienced and well-regarded agent representing you, you have a much better shot at getting ahead in a cutthroat, competitive, and overpopulated industry. But in a city flooded with an ever-increasing number of attractive, talented hopefuls, getting the attention of a good agent is a job in and of itself. You need to research agents, throw yourself into networking, send out invitations to anything you book that you want prospective agents to see you in, send emails, send postcards, and hope that something in there clicks and a decent agent decides to add you to their roster. Then your agent needs to submit you through the proper channels. . . . On and on the barriers stack up.

I had all the barriers standing between me and my goal. I lived in Seattle. I had hustled hard to ensure that I didn't have student loan debt, but that also meant I didn't have more than seven dollars in savings. I had a wife and kids. I didn't have an agent in Seattle, let alone in New York, so I couldn't find the contact information for the Broadway production's casting director. But as always, I refused to be deterred by all these barriers telling me that I couldn't do it.

My grandpa always told a story, or maybe it was a joke. An old man prayed every day to God that he would win the lottery. He wished and prayed every day of his life that he would win the lottery because not only would it help him, but it would help his children and his community. On his deathbed he had nothing; he looked up to God from his deathbed and said, "Dear God, why couldn't you have just allowed me to win the lottery?" God responded, "Why didn't you ever buy a ticket?"

We must do the work. I decided to go buy my lottery ticket.

Curious Incident is a family drama, but Christopher frames his experience of it as his own personal detective story. He investigates the killing of a neighbor's dog, which leads him to discover that despite what his father led him to believe, his mother is still alive. He then embarks on a journey to go find her, dodging police officers as he adventures through bustling train stations and unfamiliar London streets. Christopher is a Sherlock Holmes fan, and he's more comfortable processing these traumatic events by imagining himself to be a detective. Remember how I explained to you earlier that autistic people are often more comfortable interacting with the world as a character? Christopher does just that. The title of the book even comes from a quote by Holmes in the 1892 short story "The Adventure of Silver Blaze":

Gregory: Is there any other point to which you would wish to draw my attention?

Holmes: To the curious incident of the dog in the night-time.

Gregory: The dog did nothing in the night-time.

Holmes: That was the curious incident.

To get cast in *Curious Incident*, I was going to have to be a detective myself. How could I get in touch with the people in charge of casting the show if I didn't even have an agent? Broadway casting directors keep their contact information under top secret lockdown to avoid drowning in endless emails from the millions of wannabe Broadway actors in New York and across the country. Agents serve as the gatekeepers between the wannabes and the decision-makers, and I didn't have an agent, only my own detective skills. After some internet sleuthing, I found out that the lead casting director for *Curious Incident* on Broadway was named Declan. So now I had a contact name but still no contact information. I kept researching, eventually discovering that in addition to casting *Curious Incident*, Declan was the resident casting director at Lincoln Center Theater. Scouring the LCT website still didn't turn up his LCT email address, so I instead emailed an address I could find on the website. This unsuspecting ticketing office received an email with my headshot, resume, some videos of me moving in the style of the show, as well as a letter expressing why I believed I should be considered for the role. I'm sure this confused the guest services employees seeing as *Curious Incident* wasn't even playing at Lincoln Center, but at the Barrymore Theatre twenty minutes away. I knew it was a long shot, but it was my only shot. With that email, I had made one small investment in my future.

I truly believe that every week you should find one way to courageously invest in yourself. You deserve it, and more importantly, the world deserves you. The world needs what makes you different. The world needs your unique perspective. Even though my email was a long shot, I was proud of myself for planting that seed.

Days turned into weeks, and I didn't hear anything back. I went back to my normal life of making ends meet with both mundane jobs and colorful street performing, while also juggling being a family man with still pursuing an acting career in Seattle.

I never stopped dreaming about *Curious Incident*, though. Sometimes when I was walking I would leave my pennies heads up on the sidewalk or on a mailbox or fence post so that someone else would find a lucky penny. Then they would remember to have dreams, and dream of their dreams coming true.

A month and a half later, an email from the cocasting director of *Curious Incident* appeared in my inbox! She let me know that the casting team wanted me to submit a video audition for the role of Christopher. I'm not exactly sure what Christopheresque journey my initial email had gone on, from being addressed to Dan Swee care of the Lincoln Center Theater box office to being replied to by the casting director Cindy Tolan a month and a half later, but who cared, I had an audition! Despite every barrier still standing exactly where it had always been, I'd been granted an opportunity to audition for the leading role in a Broadway show. I still wasn't sure how I was going to break through the remaining barriers, but I reminded myself that you don't have to have all the answers to begin. Take one step at a time. Once you've completed the first step, you will be able to see more clearly what the second step might look like; then you will be able to see the third, and eventually you will have gotten so much further than you could have ever imagined. Than you could have ever seen.

I was so excited to share my incredible news with my friends and colleagues! But instead of celebration and congratulations, I received discouragement. Even though the Broadway casting team was warming up to the idea of an autistic actor playing this autistic role, I was sharply reminded that society at large still believed such a thing was impossible. People I looked up to in the Seattle theatre industry cautioned me that although the opera and children's theatre had been letting me play nonspeaking parts, I should know that this was a Big Show with Big Words. I suspect that not only did people around me believe that an autistic actor couldn't do the role, but they were also just plain jealous that I had secured an opportunity that all actors dream about but few ever get to experience. I couldn't even get any local actor to agree to help me with my video submission. All I needed was someone to press Record on the camera and stand off-screen reading the lines of other people Christopher was in dialogue with, but no one was willing to lend this simple assistance. Here was my chance at Broadway, but I couldn't find a colleague willing to give me less than an hour of their time in order to help me take my once-in-a-lifetime shot. I offered to pay for their time, to buy lunch, to buy gift cards . . . but couldn't find any takers. I guess everyone was either convinced that it was a hopeless case that they didn't want to waste their time on, or they were too jealous or bound by a scarcity mindset to help someone else on their way.

I am sure that scarcity mindset leads to a lack of morality. CEOs and politicians who put themselves and their profits before the health of our planet and the well-being of the most marginalized populations are, believe it or not . . . scared. They are so scared that they are stuck in a mindset that pits them against the rest of the world. Even against the environment. Instead, when we lead with courage, we are able to reimagine and expand our moral compasses. When we are courageous and value all people as being experts in something, all people as being brilliant at something, we become braver than these CEOs and politicians who put their own power first. We become more powerful, more grounded, more unshakable, using the creative brilliance of our morals to anchor us. We can choose to act out of love and selfish bravery instead of acting out of fear. You are as big and brave and intelligent as any powerful person in the world. You can be as strategic as the most powerful movers and shakers. You have the power to do great things led by love and courage, not by fear.

Who did I know, what friends did I have, who could read these scenes with me? My wife flat out refused to help. One would hope that their spouse would be their biggest fan in the world, their most reliable support and their constant cheerleader. You'd expect them to at least be supportive of you going after your dreams. At the bare minimum, you'd expect them to be all for a job that would bring in more money for the family, thus improving their own quality of life. This wasn't my experience. Eventually I did receive one lone offer of help. A Seattle actress I vaguely knew volunteered to read the sides with me, but what did I do? Chicken out. She was so beautiful and confident, and I was too shy to reply to her email. Autism strikes again. I ended up getting my dad to agree to help me film the two sides. His task wasn't difficult, and we got the video done. I uploaded the two videos and sent another hopeful email, albeit this time it was directly to the casting team, no ticketing office necessary!

The following month, *Curious Incident* won five Tony Awards and I received another email from casting, this time letting me know that if I happened to find myself in NYC in the next couple of months they would love to see me for an in-person audition in front of the show's director.

I sat silently frozen in front of my laptop, my fingers unmoving, absolutely stunned to realize that my shot in the dark had worked! Despite all the barriers in my way and the appalling lack of support from my community, I had now secured a callback for a Tony Award–winning Broadway show! Was this even *real*? Due to my impaired eyesight, sometimes my reading comprehension isn't very strong. It's difficult to see the big picture of a message when for you reading is a painstaking process that involves identifying words one letter at a time. I showed the email to Linda Hartzell, the artistic director of Seattle Children's Theatre and a rare soul in the industry who had always been kind to me. She read it and advised me to reply, stating that I had no upcoming plans to be in NYC, but I could certainly make myself available if they would be willing to fly me out to them.

It worked. I soon found myself at New York's JFK Airport, fresh off a cross-country flight that had been purchased by the *Curious Incident* team. An airport is an absolutely wild experience for an autistic person. It is overwhelming sensory input, but it's also intensely enjoyable because there is so much order to it. Everything is labeled. Everyone knows where they are going and when they need to be there. There are conveyor belts that force people to move together in the same direction. Every gate is clearly labeled and in strict alphanumeric order, and another Starbucks coffee shop is always just past the next bend in every terminal. Sometimes knowing what to expect can be so comforting. Everywhere you look, there are clocks and countless signs making sure you clearly know what is running as expected and what is not running as expected. There is a perception of autistic people that we don't do well with change, but I prefer to reframe it as we do well when we know what to expect. All's right with the world when you are an autistic person at an airport on a day when foul weather isn't toying with schedules. It is certainly loud, noisy, and overwhelming, but it's also exciting at the same time. And perfectly organized. It means the start to an adventure.

In my life I try to do one thing every day that scares me. If I do it means I am stepping out of my comfort zone and growing.

Are you making decisions in your life out of fear or out of hope, love, and strength? When you are brave, you are more capable of achieving your dreams. And you will achieve those dreams with more heart. With an unflinching moral compass.

This was my first traveling adventure that I'd ever done completely solo. I was sandwiched between total strangers on the plane, and no one was waiting for me at the airport to take me under their wing and guide me where to go next. I felt a lot like the character I was in town to audition for: completely alone as I forged ahead on an expedition into unfamiliar, hyperstimulating territory. I decided not to focus on the unknown and instead cling to something concrete. I funneled all my focus into finding and following the signs that promised to lead me to the taxis, and soon I was in the back of a cab, rolling away from the snaking line of people each waiting for a little yellow car to take them away from this place of order and into the sprawling city. After I clearly let the driver know that I was going to the Edison Hotel, I participated in my driver's interest in making small talk with me, and let him know that I was in town to audition for the lead role in *The Curious Incident of Dog in the Night-Time*, which was playing at the Barrymore Theatre. When my driver finally pulled over and said, "Here's your stop!" all I saw were the gleaming lights of the Barrymore Theatre, with bright blue *Curious Incident* imagery splashed across the marquee and on exterior walls. "No, not yet, I haven't gotten in the show yet!" I panicked, instantly feeling lost. He chuckled, pointed across the street, and reassured me with, "No, the Edison Hotel. Right there." I was gobsmacked by my luck. I had simply booked the cheapest hotel I could find in the heart of the city, trying to get as close as possible to the rehearsal space where my audition was being held. By some blessed twist of fate, it ended up being directly across the street from the theatre that the show performed in, and I had somehow never realized this when I booked it! That night from my hotel window I could see the *Curious Incident* actors leaving the stage door one by one, being met by hordes of people hoping for an autograph. I quietly stood immobilized in the window, imagining myself standing on that same pavement signing autographs in just a few short months from then. In that moment my ambitious dream felt more in reach than ever.

The next day I walked into my audition, slipping my noise-reducing headphones down from my ears to rest on either side of the V-shaped neck of my blue T-shirt. It was a rehearsal room just like any other. Well-worn flooring and bare white walls devoid of any decor. A blank canvas upon which to paint life in vivid colors of song, dance, and drama. In the room was Bentley the director, taking me in through thick-rimmed glasses that made a bold statement against his bald, translucent, egg-shaped head. Next to him was Declan, the casting director I'd originally reached out to via a ticketing office. His eyes were kind, and his smile was luminous and warm. This inviting demeanor put me instantly at ease. Next to him was cocasting director Caroline, who had been the person I'd since been emailing with. Even though her frame was small, she radiated big, powerhouse, tough love vibes. It was such a relief to be finally putting faces to the names that had been swirling in my head for many months. There was also a person there to read the lines of Christopher's scene partners, as well as a few assistants. Now, most auditions are over in a matter of minutes. You do the sides or monologue that you've prepared ahead of time, or they give you new sides to take your first stab at as a "cold read," and sometimes they might have you do all of the above. It's either done and dusted at that point, or they might give you some brief suggestions of how they'd like to see you do it again but different, and you give it another go. All in all, an audition likely takes three to five minutes. You have three to five minutes to show a casting team why you are the person they should cast in the role, and you've got to hope that by the end of the day you still stand out in their memories among the countless actors who will be doing their few minutes before and after yours. But my audition for *Curious Incident* was incredibly long by audition standards. It was also significantly different from any audition I'd ever done before then. This audition lasted one and a half hours. First they had me sit in a chair on the other side of their auditioning panel table, and they spent an entire hour simply chatting with me. In my initial email sent to the Lincoln Center box office, I described myself as having "functional" autism spectrum disorder, to allay any fears or lack of knowledge on their end. This is a *much* less than ideal term, but I needed a job. It became clear that this lengthy conversation was simply meant to determine if I'd given them an honest assessment of my social and intellectual capabilities. They wanted to make sure that I was autistic but not too autistic, whatever that means. After an hour of me just talking to these strangers, which was absolutely exhausting for an autistic person, we then moved to doing sides. I stood on an X of tape on the rehearsal room floor and read for Christopher, while the reader sat in a chair by the auditioning panel's table and said the lines of the other characters. I threw myself into the character, which admittedly wasn't too hard because he was simply a younger version of myself. Nondisabled actors win all kinds of coveted awards because everyone is so wowed by how hard they must have worked to portray a disabled person. It's not so hard when you are actually disabled. I just took the lines someone else penned and colored them in with my lived experience.

After thirty minutes of that, they let me know they'd seen all they needed to see. I thanked them for their time, they thanked me for mine, and I left not knowing if they'd ever wish to see me again. I headed back to my hotel room, then back to JFK Airport to get back to my normal life in Seattle.

Things move pretty slowly and deliberately in the professional theatre world, and they tend to happen pretty far out in advance. This meant that it wasn't until six months later that they flew me back for a final callback, this time in front of the Broadway producers. The producers are the financial backers of a production. They have a somewhat different perspective on casting, as they see through a filter of dollar signs. They are looking for the best possible return on their investment. They also don't concern themselves with the minutiae of the casting process until official decisions are about to be made. They hire casting directors to handle all that preliminary slogging through hundreds, even thousands of Broadway wannabes. So, I knew that this was the final stage. Unfortunately, my Broadway dreams had come to the end of the line, as *Curious Incident* had recently announced that the Broadway run would be coming to an end.

However, they were now looking for two actors for a thrilling opportunity to travel all around the country, taking turns performing on the upcoming national tour. Christopher is an incredibly physically demanding role that also requires you to remain onstage for almost every moment of the play, so they always double-cast the role so that the actors can have time to rest and recuperate. There were only six actors left in consideration for the two roles, and I was one of them. Of the six actors, I'm sure by now it's not surprising to hear that I was the only one who was autistic.

The first day was movement intensive, and I was beyond excited to show them my strengths! Circus skills had been my refuge and obsession throughout my whole lonely life, and I so strongly felt that it had all been in preparation for this moment. Did it really matter that I never had any friends throughout school? That just meant that I'd been left with plenty of alone time with which to practice all kinds of acrobatics, which was exactly what I now needed to be excellent at in order to secure this highly coveted, starring role of a lifetime. Nonautistic people had for years been saying that an autistic person could not play the role of Christopher Boone, and one of the reasons that was always given was the difficult movement in the show. However, I was surprised when the director walked right past the other five actors to pull me aside. He whispered in my ear, "Hey, Mickey! So good to see you! Soo . . . you don't actually need to do any of the movements if you don't want to. You can just watch." I realized in that moment that they all thought I couldn't be touched because Christopher the fictional character didn't like being touched, and Christopher had been their only touchpoint with the autistic community. The autistic community has a motto: Nothing about us without us. This means that we don't believe that stories should be told about autistic people or services provided for autistic people without autistic people being involved in the leadership and/or decision-making process. All previous iterations of *Curious Incident* had largely paid no mind to this motto. At best, they may have hired an autistic person to be an "autism consultant" who spends a day or two coaching the nonautistic actor on mimicry of some outward symptoms of autism, but that's it. At the end of the day, Christopher is merely a character made up by a nonautistic author. As much as I feel an affinity to him, I also don't. The script has him doing plenty of things that just don't ring true to me as an actually autistic person, like when Christopher barks like a dog at strangers for no apparent reason. I'm sure it all seems strange to nonautistic people, but strange to a nonautistic person doesn't mean that it's actually autistic. Autism is also a very broad spectrum, and we are not a monolith. Just because Christopher is written to be sensory avoidant does not mean that all autistic people are. In fact, many people with autism are actually sensory seeking and much more comfortable when being very physical. When doing theatre or when doing circus skills, I get to spin around and tumble and move and it makes the world very comfortable for me.

I thanked the director for the concern and willingness to make accommodations I might need, but I also assured him that I stilt walk, ride unicycles, and so much more, and that I would most definitely be doing the same audition content as everyone else. I reminded him that they had flown me out to New York to see if I could do the movement, and here I was ready to show them. Meanwhile in my internal monologue that I didn't dare to utter out loud, I questioned if they were actually considering me. How could they consider me for the role if I completely sat out the audition? Did they just want to be able to report that they had in fact actually auditioned an autistic actor? Surely not. They had spent all this time and money on flying me cross-country on two occasions. I felt more determined than ever to show them that I didn't need to sit out the movement section of the audition. I was determined to show them that not only could I do it, but I could do it better than any other actor in that room.

Now, although it was a welcome change to have a theatre interested in making accommodations for me, it gets complicated when something is less accommodation and more infantilization. Often, I will be on job interviews and people will be talking to me like I am fourteen years old, despite the fact that I'm not fourteen years old. I am a dad with two kids, who has to pay the bills and do all the things that an adult has to do.

Now you, my friend reading this book, may be feeling discouraged and wondering how the heck do you make accommodations without infantilizing?! Maybe you're frustrated at me and feeling like I've given you an impossible task. Never fear. Look to the motto of autistic people: Nothing about us without us. Rather than trying to guess what accommodations a disabled person might need, just ask them directly. And believe them when they tell you. Believe them when they tell you what they can do and what they cannot do. Trust that they are the experts on their own lives. If you're not sure if you can ask them—maybe they're a child or nonspeaking—ask another adult with the same disability. This callback could easily have gotten off to a smoother start if ahead of time the team had reached out to me via email with something like, "Do you have any access needs, or are there any accommodations we can make for you on the day of the callback?" See the difference? They unexpectedly offered me something that they decided by themselves might be helpful for me, but it actually wasn't helpful at all. What would have been even better would have been asking me directly ahead of time if there was anything that might be helpful. Make sense? You got this, my friend. Go forth with confidence!

After we got past that clunky interaction, the rubber hit the road. All six of us potential Christophers were in the room together working with each other, not against each other. Sometimes there can be a toxic, competitive atmosphere in a group callback, but this felt pretty collaborative. It probably helped that we knew there were two roles up for grabs on the same tour. It would be unwise to try to screw someone over now, as you may very well end up stuck on tour with them for the foreseeable future. The choreographer taught us all the movement in the show, but broken up into drills. Holding planks for ten minutes, then doing jumping jacks and crunches, then holding a side plank for ten minutes. Repeat, repeat, repeat. Sprinting around the room. More planks. And then, then we got to fly! Lifted by the other five actors in the room, I flew around the space like an astronaut. I was sky high in the room and in my feelings, finally days away from achieving the dream I had been working for over two years on. Lifted by another actor pressing his weight into my shoulder, I walked on the wall, my body parallel to the floor. One of the other actors stood next to me, his arm outreached, pressing into my shoulder and my arm pressing into his shoulder. He leaned into me as I slowly, carefully, placed one of my feet onto the wall. Then another. Placing one foot in front of the other, I walked up the wall until I was sideways, completely parallel with the floor! In front of me was the producers' table, only sideways. It appeared to be on the wall, with all the producers, casting directors, and associates sitting calmly behind their table, not noticing that the room had turned sideways and their chairs were now affixed to the wall! I walked toward them. Holding my plank. The whole room on its side.

Placing my entire foot on the wall heel to toe for the maximum grip I could muster. The sweat that dripped off me didn't run down my face to the floor beneath my feet but fell off my body sideways as if being whisked away by a sudden perpendicular wind or burst of sideways gravity from some space-age machine hidden in the ground to my side. The visual looked as surreal as this whole day felt. And they wanted me to sit this out. . . .

After a full day of intense physical activity, the five other potential Christophers were released to go spend the rest of the night recuperating and preparing however they wished before the final day of auditions for the producers. The casting team had other plans for me. That night they had me sitting dead center in the second row of the Barrymore Theatre, watching the show while the director watched me. It was clear they just wanted to see if the show would be too much for me and my sensory processing disorder to handle, what with all the theatre magic bells and whistles such as strobing lights and sudden eruptions of sound. The show ends with Christopher exclaiming, "Confetti!" and paper petals exploding into a rainstorm onto the audience. It was quite a strange experience to have to act natural while someone is clearly side-eye analyzing you through multicolored rain. I made sure to smile Very Broadly and clap very loudly even though I had spent the last three hours watching a nonautistic actor play every autistic stereotype under the sun to an applauding nondisabled audience. Also, I suspect anyone, autistic or not, would find it very awkward to watch a show while sitting next to the show's director.

It's the same situation as when a new parent places their newborn in your arms. They will always then give you an earnest yet expectant look, and no matter what you actually think you have to say how beautiful you think their baby is. And at any rate, it was such an unbalanced power dynamic. I'm sitting next to the director as we watch his show that I want him to cast me in. Me wanting this job makes my honest feedback neither wanted nor helpful in that moment. The only thing I can do to keep myself in the running for this job is simply to smile Very Broadly and clap very loudly. Finally, the last piece of confetti fluttered to the ground and the audience members waddled together through the seats and out to the lobby of the theatre.

Finally, I was free to go. It seemed to happen right as all the other Broadway shows were releasing their audiences out into the night as well. The walk back to my hotel room was a slog through the biggest traffic jam of my life. Construction projects had left half of the sidewalks in the vicinity of Times Square closed. It was a crush of humanity. Chests touching backs, backs touching chests, people inching along. I could hardly breathe.

Tuck thumb into fist, squeeze once, squeeze twice, keep walking. Squeeze. Squeeze. Squeeze. Step. Step. Step. I eventually made it back to my hotel room and promptly collapsed into my bed. It had been an extraordinarily long day, and in just a few short hours I'd be waking up and heading back into a room with five other potential Christophers, all of them better rested than I and all of them nonautistic.

The next day was the final callback. All of the producers were there, tight lipped and all business. The six actors were brought into the room one at a time to do a scene, and then we were free to go. For four of us, this would mark the end of our *Curious Incident* journeys. We'd go back to our previous hustles, forever knowing that we were so close and yet so far. The other two would be going on a national tour. I knew my odds were pretty good at this point. Since the role was double-cast, I had a one-in-three chance.

"Be fearless in the pursuit of your dreams. Be courageous in the pursuit of what you know is right," I told myself.

When it was my turn in front of the producers, they let me know that I was the only autistic actor they had ever even seen. I think they meant this as a compliment, but to me it felt immensely complex. Firstly, it meant that deep down they did not care about authentic representation. If at any point they'd had any interest in having the producers see more autistic people audition, they could have taken simple action and made that happen. The release of a single audition notice saying as such would have been responded to with hundreds of submissions. Instead they passively waited until one lone autistic actor sent a long-shot email to the ticketing office of a theatre that wasn't even doing the show but just happened to be another place where the casting director worked. One lone autistic person had to go through such great lengths in order to get their attention, whereas they so easily could have solicited submissions from hundreds of autistic actors. Furthermore, the producers said I was the only autistic actor they had *ever seen*. I can't help but assume that this encompassed not just this show, but any show they'd ever produced.

One in fifty-four people are autistic, and I assure you that plenty of autistic people work in theatre, although they may not feel safe enough to publicize their diagnosis. You, reader of this book, are now well acquainted with all the reasons one might find it safer to keep their diagnosis a secret. How many autistic people had the producers actually unknowingly seen before me over the course of their careers, but the actors simply didn't dare jeopardize their already slim chances by divulging their diagnosis? This also made me wonder exactly what I'd pondered the day before, when they offered to let me sit out and not perform the audition content. Was I actually being given a fair shot here? Was I actually being considered for the role? What if all this had simply been a performative act, to make them feel forever immune to any criticism from the disability community? Now they could always say that of course they are inclusive; they had an autistic person make it all the way to final callbacks. I am sure this director meant it as a compliment when they told me I was the only autistic actor they had ever seen. I am also sure that they had no idea of the layers of complexities built into that admission. But I steeled myself and let all the complexities evaporate from my consciousness. If the producers were going to see only one autistic person, then thank God it would be me.

I dove into the scene, feeling my dream pressing in on me with only a thin, transparent veil between us now. I spoke the last lines of the play. The lines uttered by Christopher after he beats the odds, gets accepted into college, overcomes his family's drama, and is living independently. "Does this mean I can do anything?" The last lines of the play. I paused and looked up. I slowly let my gaze move across the room, making eye contact with each of the people who had been a part of my journey so far. I thought on my grandma, who had now passed away. I thought on Linda at SCT. I tasted salt as a single tear made contact with my lip. Does this mean I can do anything? My audition was done. I thanked everyone for their time and gave them each a handwritten thank-you card. They thanked me for my time, I nodded and then headed for the door, not knowing if I'd ever see any of them again. I left aflame with excitement and possibility. I knew that tomorrow my dream would have either officially come true or it would be over, and that was comforting for me. Autistic people do well when we know what to expect, and with only two possible outcomes there weren't too many variables to worry about.

This time my walk back to the hotel through New York City streets felt empty and quiet. I feel most at home walking the streets of a city where nobody knows me. Going for a walk around downtown Seattle had long been a refuge for me from an unhappy, unhealthy marriage and home life. Apparently, some people throw themselves into affairs or alcohol to cope with unhappy marriages, but I was partial to a quiet, solitary, incognito walk in a big city. Much less destructive, and truer to my nature. So that quiet, solitary, incognito walk through an even bigger city was a welcome refuge from the turbulent last two days of producer callbacks.

As expected, the next day my phone buzzed and lit up. The casting director's name flashed across the screen. Did I dare pick up? This was my last moment of not knowing. Two years of work, hopes, and dreams for this. Two years of this being my one shot. Two years of not knowing were reduced to this one final moment. I knew that when I got off this call I would either be soaring at the heights of elation or crushed in heartbreaking defeat. But in this moment of unknowing, I could still exist in a comfortable place at neither end of the emotional spectrum. I let it buzz one more time, one more moment of unknowing, before I answered the phone, barely breathing enough to release an audible, "Hello?"

I remember only one thing that they said on the call. They offered to me that when the show came to Seattle, they would get me into the audience and let me go backstage afterward to take my picture with the cast. I'm sure they meant well, but it felt like such a slap in the face. People with autism don't just want to be audience members. We don't want to be superficially included as mere observers. We want to be employed. We want to be leaders in the conversation.

I was too distracted by the feeling of my heart sinking through my chest, through my feet, and down through the floor of the hotel room to remember anything else that was said on that call. It felt like my heart fell straight through all thirty-six floors of the hotel just to shatter on the granite floor in the lobby under the close observation of the dozens of tourists on their way out to fancy dinner dates. I didn't hear anything else. It doesn't really matter what was said, though. The implications were that the producers had decided it would be easiest to cast a nonautistic actor. The producers had done that many times before in London and now in New York. It was easy. Didn't take a lot of creativity. Didn't take critical thinking or learning. It didn't take any imagination. It was easy. Easy for them, at least. Now a nonautistic actor would have to figure out how to mimic autism. That's hard. Easy would have been an actually autistic person being autistic onstage. But that would have been different for the producers, and different is scary and scary is not easy. People are so scared of things that are different, and people are absolutely terrified of things that they don't understand.

But money! People sure understand money, and gosh, do they love it! *Curious Incident* had won the Tony Award for Best Play and was an exceedingly lucrative cash cow. It took just over three months on Broadway for the show's producers to have recouped their entire investment. They were making plenty of money with nonautistic actors in cripface. Why would they take a gamble on accurate representation? Much safer for them to keep profiting off autism without actually employing any autistic people.

The brighter your light, the more people will work to put it out. Don't let them. They are just angry that they don't allow their own light to shine so brightly. As poet Arch Hades says, "Some people will hate you when they see in you, what is missing in them, and they will try to pick you apart for it, because that's easier than working on themselves."

In that second it was all gone. I was so stupid to work so hard for this. To believe I could do it. People sometimes say I'm not the brightest penny in the till.

Every once in a while, I like climbing the highest trees and then, once I'm at the top, just letting go, balancing for a little because it's like taking my life out of my hands and putting it up for fate. It's like saying, "Hey, God. I'm not even sure if you really exist or not, but I'm gonna put my life in your hands for a little bit. But it's cool; I trust you."

Sometimes I think that if we only trusted a little bit more, then we would all also be more trustworthy in return, making people trust even more on top of that. Like a domino set or one of those butterflies in South America that can cause a hurricane or something. Maybe instead of "all you need is love," the song should have gone, "all you need is trust" because I know lots of people who have hurt and abused those that they honestly and truly loved the most.

My mind began to flutter out of control.

I want to make it clear that the casting directors and casting team were never anything but kind, courteous, and full of love, and casting directors do not get the final say in casting, contrary to popular belief. They took me as far as they had the power to. Declan and Caroline are both incredible, smart, and kind people.

Risk. Fail. Risk again. If you are not failing, you are not learning. If you are not allowed to fail, you are not allowed to learn and grow.

At the same time, I was reminded of the old saying: The child who is not embraced by the village will burn it down to feel its warmth. I didn't want this to be me!

It took about six hours to fly back to Seattle from New York, which was a long time to spend with nothing to do but sit with reality. I hadn't gotten the show. My adventure had ended. I worked as a dishwasher for much of the next year, did my best to de-escalate an increasingly volatile home life, and neither the Broadway production, West End production, nor the national tour ever cast an autistic actor.

9

The person who says it cannot be done should not interrupt the person doing it.

—Confucius

A t twenty-eight I could have been in a different city every week, performing the lead role in a Tony Award–winning play upon whatever the city of the week's grandest stage was. My wife and children would get to live it up in my hotel rooms across the country for a full year or more. No rent, housekeeping taking care of nearly everything, exploring national parks and new cities on my four days off per week, what a carefree life!

Instead, at twenty-eight years old I was washing dishes for a living, with my wife trapped at home by agoraphobia, her brain wracked with so much anxiety that it made her refuse to even let me hold my own baby.

This wasn't the plan.

At twenty-four years old, I'd still only had the one girlfriend and a few friends with benefits. I met girls from working in the theatre industry, as well as online. In December of that year I met someone with a color for a name through an online dating site. Grey. Weird. Well, okay. I'd had some even weirder experiences with girls I'd met online, like the one time some girl told me she genuinely believed I was Jesus or another who told me she was a witch who could cast spells. This girl's name just happened to be the name of a drab color. That's not so weird. We met for our first date at a gas station in front of her parents' house then took the bus to my apartment while eating out of a plastic grocery bag the popcorn she had popped for us.

I had thought that the plan was just a hookup date, which was usually all that girls wanted with me, but was pleasantly surprised by the rare find of a girl who afterward expressed interest in us seeing each other again and getting to know each other more. It had been two years since things had amicably ended with my first girlfriend Anika, the Nordic hippie, due to college and I hadn't had a girlfriend since, so I was excited and ready to explore entering into another relationship.

Very early on in our relationship I let her know about my eyesight and autism diagnosis. I wanted to be sure she knew before she got too attached. To my surprise and great relief, she didn't have an opinion about it either way. I was so used to always being stigmatized, rejected, or infantilized whenever I shared with anyone that I was autistic. It felt really new and reassuring to have someone whose feelings for me didn't change when she found out I was autistic. She let me know about her ongoing mental health struggles with bipolar disorder and psychosis and the meds she took to manage them, which truly didn't faze me at all. I strongly believed that mental health issues shouldn't be stigmatized, in the same way that physical health issues and disability shouldn't be stigmatized. She was taking her meds and seeing her therapists, so I was neither concerned nor turned off. I felt warmed by mutual acceptance between us, and my future looked bright with hope.

We moved in together a month and a half after our first date because neither of us could afford rent on our own and splitting the cost of an apartment seemed like the best solution. Her anxiety sometimes manifested as agoraphobia, and she stopped working when it started getting the best of her. I cheerfully took up bearing the entire rent bill, figuring it was just doing my part as a supportive boyfriend to get her through a brief rough patch. She brought up the subject of marriage very early on, which came as a surprise to me. Remember, this had begun just a few weeks earlier as a casual hookup. But over a lifetime of being disabled I'd been conditioned to fear that this could be the only time someone would ever be interested in marrying me. I remember one day while taking a shower hearing a bloodcurdling scream that reached me through the bathroom door, cutting through the pounding water pummeling the bathtub floor and shower curtain. I ran into the living room, leaving wet footprints down the carpeted hallway. I could feel the beads of water still running down my legs as she yelled at me from behind her laptop that the ring she wanted had gone on sale and I needed to give her my debit card *now*! A few days later it arrived in our mailbox. Any chances of me pulling off a surprise proposal were clearly shot by that point, but I figured I'd better make as much of a special moment out of it as I could. We drove about forty-five minutes east of Seattle, and with a waterfall's cold spray misting down on us I got down on one knee and asked her to marry me. Unsurprisingly, she said yes, put on the ring she'd purchased online, and we drove back home. We began planning for a wedding in August of 2013, which was a mere nine months after our first date.

We made all the decorations ourselves because we couldn't afford to buy any. There was Elmer's glue all over the carpet of our apartment from sticking hand-cut burlap triangles onto a cream-colored ribbon: our own elementary school craft project version of bunting. We decided to have our wedding in a public park to save money. My bride-to-be took a piece of paper and drew a map of where she wanted everything to go. I didn't have the heart to tell her that the spot she picked was right by the dock where I'd done the deed with my first girlfriend.

The day came, and I arrived early in the morning to set everything up by myself. She was getting ready at her parents' house, my family was entertaining guests who'd flown in from overseas for my wedding, and I still didn't really have any friends. I didn't even have groomsmen to stand with me on my wedding day. So I hung my suit up on a tree branch, put on my headphones, and got to work bringing her hand-drawn map to life. It was a rare sunny day in Seattle, and I'm the kind of white that just burns. No lingering pit stop at tan, I just go straight from pink to red. Single-handedly setting up an outdoor wedding? *Boy, did I burn.*

She had grand plans for the park's giant wood picnic tables to be lined up to create one long farmhouse-style banquet table, with our hand-glued burlap table runner lying down the middle. I discovered that morning that although the picnic tables looked very portable, their rounded steel frames made them incredibly heavy. But the little map jeered at my limitations and told me that weight was irrelevant. The picnic tables were expected to be assembled into a long line, and so in a long line they would be. So with sweat staining outward from the V of my shirt, I got to work. If any park staff later wondered where to locate the picnic tables that were usually scattered across the park, they could just follow the gashes that were torn into the grass as a lone figure pushed, pulled, and dragged them into a line by a certain dock. Oh, the crimes I have committed against this respectable park.

My cruel master of a map next ordered that the homemade bunting had to be made to span the two trees in the field. It wasn't until I was partway into my climb of the first tree that I discovered that the trees were covered in thorns. I wiped a bead of sweat off my sunburned forehead and left a smear of blood in its place. Dammit, I was bleeding. *Eff this effing bunting. Eff this effing WEDDING!* I clung to the thorny tree and weighed my options. I still had time to run. Ugh, but I had most likely lost my apartment deposit due to the Elmer's debacle. Why did no one realize till now that even the most luxurious bunting we could buy off Amazon would still have cost less than a deposit equal to one month's rent? Rent! The rent that I was still single-handedly footing the bill for because she still had too much anxiety to go to work. And here I was, single-handedly setting up an outdoor wedding to exactly her specifications. The only help she or anyone else was giving me with it was just this stupid effing scrawl of a map. Breathe in. Breathe out. Tuck my thumb inside a fist and squeeze once, twice. Breath. Breath. Breath. There was a girl who wanted to marry me, and she wanted this bunting strung between two thorny trees while she did. I decided in that moment that come hell or high water I was going to hang up the damn bunting and marry the damn girl.

Finally, everything was as the map had ordered. Burlap bunting flapped between the two thorny trees. More burlap lay along the hulking line of picnic tables. At the head of the table sat a grocery store cake, crowned with a flower. Earlier that day I'd stopped by Seattle's world-famous Pike Place Market, with the map holding a gun to my head and threateningly whispering in my ear that I needed to purchase every purple and every white flower from every flower seller and farmer there was. The cake had bounced on the car ride to the park, hitting the top of the shallow box the teenage grocery store employee had put it in. So, I plopped a large purple hydrangea on top of the cake to cover the squished spot, and that's the story behind the cake's flower crown. Surely this was what was meant by the phrase a "fool's errand."

Burlap fibers tickled my nose, but trying to remove them was an exercise in futility, as the hands I wiped them with were also covered in fibers. I was absolutely covered in sweat, blood, sunburn, and rogue strands of burlap. I checked the time on my phone. Shit! Everyone would be showing up soon. I couldn't get married looking like this. My eyes desperately scoured the park for a shower block, but I couldn't see anything. *Shit shit shit.* My searching eyes landed on the dock where I'd gotten naked just a few years earlier.

I think people traditionally go skinny-dipping at their bachelor party instead of minutes before their wedding, but I bet those bachelors also have it arranged for other people to set up their wedding. Standing in front of our handful of guests, all I knew was that lake water may cool you down but it certainly doesn't leave you feeling clean. I was quite the uncomfortable groom: lake washed, scratched, and sunburned under a summer sun while wearing a suit and tie. Part of the reason why I wear V-necked shirts so often is because I don't like the sensation of something touching my neck. But on that particular day, the purple tie was truly the least of my discomfort concerns. Grey walked down the aisle toward me, we said words and made promises, but I just wanted to go home, take a shower with soap, maybe rub some Neosporin on my cuts and aloe vera gel on my burns. Then just like that, we kissed, and I became a husband. *Hey. I did it!* I had a wife. I may have felt distracted by discomfort through our ceremony, but I did mean every word that I had promised her, and I was fully committed to living out those promises till the day I died.

Two days later we were in the car, off to run some errand. We hadn't had money to go on a honeymoon so life as usual had chugged on, but now with the new constant sensation of a wedding band encircling my finger. My wife's voice suddenly broke the silence. I don't remember exactly what she said, but I clearly remember my own confusion and a growing sense of entrapment as she let me know she intended to start a family right away. I felt instantly taken back to less than a year before, in the early days of dating when she had quickly begun pressuring me into marriage. Here we were, two days married, and she was letting me know for the first time that she wanted to have children as soon as possible. While we'd previously discussed an openness to having children one day, this was the first I'd heard of an immediate wish for them. Soon after, she began pestering me up to five times a day to get her pregnant. I finally relented when she gave a cruel ultimatum: if I did not get her pregnant in the next two months, then she would go get pregnant by someone else, and I would never even know about it.

Our firstborn son, let's call him "A," arrived the following summer.

He barely slept, and as he grew into a toddler I started noticing him showing other signs of autism. When I took "A" to toddler music classes he would cover his ears. He wouldn't pick up on the social cues of kids who didn't want to play with him on the playground, often insisting they play with him rather than understanding their cues and respecting their own bodily autonomy.

The most current research is determining that autism is largely genetic, passed down by the father. By this point my wife had begun daily calling me a "retard" and made it clear that she wished she didn't have an autistic husband. I was highly concerned about how she'd handle receiving an autism diagnosis for her son also. But like any parent, I wanted my child to have a better life than I'd had. I decided that if he was indeed autistic, getting a diagnosis would help him access supports we might need at school to ensure his greatest success.

The first step was getting on a waiting list for him to be seen by the University of Washington Autism Clinic, the same place his dad had gone for his diagnosis just a few years before. After waiting for six months we finally received an appointment and were sent thick packets of papers, questionnaires, multiple-choice questions, 1-out-of-10 bubble scoring sheets to be filled out by his father, his mother, and the head of his day care. When I was diagnosed as an adult, the diagnosis process was much faster, which makes sense as you are answering questions about yourself. For my three-year-old, it was a three-day process. The first day involved my wife and me meeting with the diagnosing doctor and going over our answers to all of these questions without our son present. She was a small lady who appeared elderly but also was sharply intelligent and articulate. Being autistic myself, I already understood the reason for each of her question, and knew, for example, when she asked about music or light, she was actually asking about sensory processing disorder, and when she asked about repetitive movement, she was actually asking about stimming. She made me feel like she was truly listening and thoughtfully considering all we shared with her. The second day involved him going on his own to "play" a series of tests and games with the doctor, as well as play in different styles. The third day was diagnosis day. The room in which I had received my diagnosis looked like a trendy living room, but this room looked like a small preschool classroom, with a round, gray laminate-top table, plastic stacking chairs with metal legs, and a plastic seat, four rounded vent slots going down the back of the seat. There was a mat on the floor, with blocks and other unstructured play toys in the corner. It was just the parents again at this meeting, without our son. I went to hold my wife's hand as reassurance, but she sat tight lipped, arms crossed tightly in front of her chest. The doctor confirmed what I had long expected to be true: autism spectrum disorder.

Having a child diagnosed with autism can feel devastating for many families, but for me it was intensely galvanizing. Like any parent, I had always been determined to give my son a better life than I'd had. Now that I officially knew that he was autistic like me, a new specificity to this mission was birthed in me. No longer was I trying to make a more equitable world for a vague, faceless community of autistic people, or even a better world just for myself. I knew that I had to do everything I could to make society more equitable for autistic people for the sake of my son. I believe that people can begin to make change in the world when they start right where they are, with the skills that they have. Acting was my skill, and when soon after I received word that the rights had opened up for *Curious Incident* to be performed by professional regional theatres around the country, I was determined to plunge back into Christopher's world and get myself cast. There was still a chance for me to be the first autistic actor cast in the role, which I hoped would be a stepping-stone into a new world of speaking engagements and media coverage. It could be a chance to have an autistic voice broadcast and amplified, and a chance to show an unbelieving world that autistic people are capable of telling their own stories and capable of speaking for themselves. And then perhaps my son would be able to tell his own stories and speak for himself.

It is always the darkest right before you succeed. When things look the darkest, do not give up. This is when you have to be the strongest. The most anchored by your moral compass, creativity, compassion, and courage. Like jumping off a diving board, courage gets easier every time you do it. You will get better at courageously investing in yourself the more you do it. The more you fail. Risk. Fail. Risk again.

Because of all the seeds I had planted during my three years of work toward *Curious Incident* on Broadway, and with a push I rallied from the disability community, I got an email from the first two professional regional productions of *Curious* given permission to do the show in the United States. They both said that I did not need to fly out to audition for them but instead asked me to film myself doing scenes from the show to send to them. This was easy since I already had half the play memorized. After watching the videos, they were both still interested, and both productions called my longtime employer Seattle Children's Theatre to ask about me. The wheels turned a little faster at one of the theatres, and they quickly asked if I would meet with the director of the show if they flew her out to Seattle. I agreed, with a growing sense of the dream pressing back in on me.

We met the very next week and spent an hour in a large-windowed rehearsal room at SCT, looking out on the Space Needle while we talked. She asked to see me do each of the sides I had videotaped to make sure the videotape wasn't just some fluke. She had me do some movement work, playing with moving doors and pens and notepads. And the next day, I got an offer to be the first autistic actor to play Christopher Boone in *The Curious Incident of the Dog in the Night-Time*, taking me all the way across the country! To Indianapolis. To New York. This would also make me one of the very first autistic actors to ever play any autistic character professionally. Like a first kiss, firsts open up a whole new world of possibilities.

A small boy (Mickey Rowe) in an orange life jacket and pirate hat on a raft that looks like a ship complete with ropes and white-sheet sails. (Note: All images include descriptions for blind and low-vision readers.)

A small boy (Mickey Rowe) in clown makeup wearing a pink paper triangular hat and a yellow tissue paper collar beside pink balloons.

A smiling ten-year-old Mickey in a rust-colored vest backstage at the Seattle Opera.

Mickey standing ten feet tall on stilts at a farmers' market wearing a black top hat, white shirt, and long black pants. The photo is taken from behind him with the farmers' market tents and a small child in front of him.

Indiana Repertory Theatre's 2017 production of *The Curious Incident of the Dog in the Night-Time*. Photo by Zach Rosing. Directed by Risa Brainin, scenic design by Russel Metheny, costumes by Devon Painter, lighting by Michael Klaers, sound by Todd Mack Reischman, projections by Katherine Freer, music composed by Michelle DiBucci, and movement by Mariel Greenlee. Gail Rastofer and Mickey Rowe stand onstage with a glassy blue wall lit with stars behind them. They are looking down at a black poodle lying on the stage between their feet.

Indiana Repertory Theatre's 2017 production of *The Curious Incident of the Dog in the Night-Time*. Photo by Zach Rosing. Mickey Rowe stands on a metal chair. The stage around him is lit with stars. He is wearing a red T-shirt, the character Christopher's favorite color.

Indiana Repertory Theatre's 2017 production of *The Curious Incident of the Dog in the Night-Time*. Photo by Zach Rosing. Elizabeth Ledo sits onstage reading from a book while Mickey Rowe balances on a chair, appearing to be floating in zero gravity.

Indiana Repertory Theatre's 2017 production of *The Curious Incident of the Dog in the Night-Time*. Photo by Zach Rosing. Elizabeth Ledo sits on a table reading from a book as Mickey Rowe sits onstage leaned up against the table. Behind them standing in a row is the cast dressed in gray. The stage is dark.

Indiana Repertory Theatre's 2017 production of *The Curious Incident of the Dog in the Night-Time*. Photo by Zach Rosing. Mickey Rowe sits onstage in a red T-shirt and light-colored jeans as Robert Neal in plaid looks at him while adjusting Rowe's shirt.

Indiana Repertory Theatre's 2017 production of *The Curious Incident of the Dog in the Night-Time*. Photo by Zach Rosing. Rowe sits center stage in a spotlight. His hand is on his jaw, and he looks as though he has been injured.

Indiana Repertory Theatre's 2017 production of *The Curious Incident of the Dog in the Night-Time*. Mickey Rowe stands in a red jacket with a backpack on and a small animal-carrying case at his side. Around him, David Alan Anderson, Gail Rastofer, and Margaret Daly stand silhouetted in the theatre's colorful side lights creating the image of a busy train station.

Indiana Repertory Theatre's 2017 production of *The Curious Incident of the Dog in the Night-Time*. Mickey Rowe is wearing a red jacket and a backpack. He holds up a white pet rat, showing it to Margaret Daly who is wearing a red plaid jacket and is carrying a brown reusable grocery bag.

Indiana Repertory Theatre's 2017 production of *The Curious Incident of the Dog in the Night-Time*. Rowe sits onstage in front of Constance Macy, who is sitting above him on a bench.

Indiana Repertory Theatre's 2017 production of *The Curious Incident of the Dog in the Night-Time*. On a subway set, Rowe hangs upside down on a handrail as Margaret Daly stands beside him.

Indiana Repertory Theatre's 2017 production of *The Curious Incident of the Dog in the Night-Time*. On a set that looks like a train populated by the cast, David Alan Anderson is dressed as a police officer with a bright yellow reflective vest. He stands with Rowe, who is wearing the red jacket and backpack. There is a glassy translucent waist-high wall.

Indiana Repertory Theatre's 2017 production of *The Curious Incident of the Dog in the Night-Time*. A yellow-striped waist-high trough runs all the way across the stage. In it is Rowe holding a white pet rat high above his head. Landon Woodson (in a suit) and Mehry Eslaminia (dressed as a punk girl with a red-and-blue-tipped Mohawk) appear on the set looking on.

Indiana Repertory Theatre's 2017 production of *The Curious Incident of the Dog in the Night-Time*. The set is completely lit with stars and galaxies. Rowe appears to be floating away as Robert Neal looks on.

Indiana Repertory Theatre's 2017 production of *The Curious Incident of the Dog in the Night-Time*. Rowe is lying on his back wearing a white shirt with red stripes, red shoes, and jeans as a small golden retriever puppy stands on top of him, licking his face. Robert Neal looks on, smiling.

Mickey and Helen, an interabled couple, hold hands as they walk along a sunlit sidewalk. He wears a gray blazer, white shirt, and jeans. She wears a scarf, red leather jacket, and black pants. Behind them are brick walls and glassy storefronts, and in the distance stands a tree with its leaves turned yellow for fall.

Helen and Mickey standing on a rooftop with the city behind them. She is wearing a black dress and a gray jacket. He is wearing a blue suit. She holds his arm with her head on his shoulder.

Helen, wearing a white dress and faux fur, leans her head into Mickey, who is wearing a black sequin houndstooth tuxedo.

Mickey Rowe dressed as a fool in oversized trousers, a vest, an oversized ruff, and a black wool felt hat, holds a skull like Hamlet might in Shakespeare's famous play.

Mickey Rowe, dressed as a fool in oversized trousers, a vest, and a black top hat, holds a tall unicycle and different juggling knives. A brick wall and props are behind him.

Syracuse Stage's 2020 production of *Amadeus*. Directed by Robert Hupp, scenic design by Misha Kachman, costumes by Tracy Dorman, lighting by Dawn Chiang, sound by Victoria Deiorio, hair and wig design by Robert Pickens. Photo by Mike Davis. Mickey Rowe and Lisa Helmi Johanson sit onstage in opulent eighteenth-century wardrobe in front of a table of colorful and delicious-looking treats.

Syracuse Stage's 2020 production of *Amadeus*. Photo by Mike Davis. Mickey Rowe sits onstage, laughing with his hand in the air while wearing a bright candy-colored jacket and a cotton candy blue eighteenth-century wig.

Syracuse Stage's 2020 production of *Amadeus*. Photo by Mike Davis. Rowe is lit in blue, standing in the foreground onstage, conducting as the cast sits lit in warm colors watching in the background.

Syracuse Stage's 2020 production of *Amadeus*. Photo by Mike Davis. Jason O'Connell wears a dark cloak while holding Mickey Rowe's cheek. Rowe appears broken and in tears.

Syracuse Stage's 2020 production of *Amadeus*. Photo by Mike Davis. Rowe stands on a gold-leafed chair, jumping up and down in pleasure surrounded by Jason O'Connell, Bill Christ, and J. D. Webster, who look on disapprovingly.

Syracuse Stage's 2020 production of *Amadeus*. Photo by Mike Davis. Mickey Rowe sits in a chair as J. D. Webster talks down to him. Bill Christ stands behind, looking disapproving.

Syracuse Stage's 2020 production of *Amadeus*. Photo by Mike Davis. Mickey Rowe crouches at a table. His hair is brown and curly and disheveled. He is writing. On the table is a bottle of wine and a lit candle.

10

Our differences are our strengths.

—Mickey Rowe

A t long last, my dream had finally broken through every barrier. After over three years of being the only person who believed it was possible and even after experiencing my dream being crushed like an empty tin can, my dream had finally come true. Not in the way that I thought it would, but I have found that you can always make your dreams come true, though rarely in the way you first imagine them or in the timeline you first expected. It requires you to be confident in your own self-worth, regardless of what anyone else says. After being rejected by society, even by my own mother, it would be so easy to be a shell. But the world doesn't need another shell of a person. The world needs you at your fullest, because of and not in spite of your "weaknesses." Your fullest doesn't mean perfect. It doesn't mean only when you've got everything all figured out and you're feeling qualified and ready. It just means your full commitment to being brave and presenting your authentic self in the moment that you are in. When you are honest with the world about who you are, you are also being honest with yourself about who you are. Only then are you able to honestly assess for yourself what your dreams actually are.

I had begun this journey wanting to be the first autistic actor to play Christopher Boone, and I figured that meant I would have to be cast in the Broadway or national tour productions of *Curious Incident*. My dream had ended up landing on a relatively small professional regional production that would open in Indiana, perform there for a while, and then ship off to Syracuse, New York, where it would close out its run. Nevertheless, I was still going to be the first autistic actor to play Christopher, and also one of the first autistic actors to play any autistic role professionally ever, dating back past *Rain Man*, through *Atypical*, *The Good Doctor*, and more.

Corporate Broadway couldn't cast inclusively, but our communities in Indiana, in Syracuse, in Louisville, in Kansas City, and in Sarasota were saying yes, we can. The first two professional regional productions of *Curious Incident* were trying to beat each other out to cast me. I accepted the first offer, but it had been quickly followed with an offer from the other coproduction. It was such a vastly different experience than what I'd had with Broadway, and it reminds me of the power of ordinary people all across our country. We can refuse to do things the way the powers that be have always unethically done them. We may not be able to change corrupt ways of doing things at the highest levels of society right away, but we can make change at whatever place it is that we find ourselves, wherever we are now, and let that snowball roll on from there. Letting that snowball be pushed further and further by ordinary people. I thought it was so refreshing and remarkable that these theatre companies weren't dissuaded by the fact that all previous, bigger-budget, award-winning productions had cast nonautistic actors. They believed that casting an autistic actor was the right thing to do, and so they were determined to do so.

You don't need to have all the answers to begin doing the right thing. These theatres could have so easily said, "Yes, we want to do *Curious Incident of the Dog in the Night-Time* and cast an actually autistic actor. We don't currently know anything about autism, so we will just add it to our goals list, begin learning about autism and then, one day in the future when we feel like we know enough about autism to not get in trouble, we will produce the show casting a disabled actor." Instead they said, "We do not know anything about autism, we know that we are going to make mistakes, but we can't let that fear stop us from doing the work. Our not knowing is not an excuse not to begin. Our not knowing is not an excuse not to try. We don't exactly know what is on the other side of this pool, but we are going to be brave, take a risk, and jump off that diving board anyway, led by our hearts and the unshakable knowledge of what is right, listening to and being led by the disability community, by the lived experience and knowledge of the actor we have cast."

Boy, did their brave choice pay off!

I was still working as a dishwasher two weeks after the casting had been announced when *boom*. A tremendous tornado of a press storm came rushing in. Now, this press didn't happen because of any press release sent by the theatres. The theatres didn't send press releases to anyone outside of their local paper. Why would they? They had always just sent the releases to the local papers. Why change when that is how things had always been done? But my own struggles in life had taught me that something always being done a certain way is not the same thing as that being the right way to do it. So as soon as the casting had been made public, I had taken the liberty of sending emails and press releases to journalists across the nation. This press storm happened because I went courageously after my goal of making a more equitable world for my autistic son. It happened because I made noise on behalf of the 20 percent of the population that had been told to disappear. The press storm happened because I was determined for the world to see that autistic people can speak for themselves and tell their own stories.

Before the show had even begun rehearsing, I was behind a microphone in dark recording booths in Seattle, speaking across the country to NPR, CNN, PBS, *Teen Vogue*, *HuffPost*, *Playbill*, BBC, the *Wall Street Journal*, and more. The press didn't even know yet if I was going to be any good in this role. We were still months from opening night. But the simple fact that an autistic actor had been cast in this role was so groundbreaking that it kicked off a steady stream of countless interviews that continued on well after the show had closed. This small production received more acclaim and press attention than both the Broadway replacement cast and the national tour put together! It was a true press storm! An unseasonably severe and utterly unaccountable storm.

One of these journalists, Matthew Rozsa, was even autistic! Matthew wrote, "For once, an autistic role will be played by an autistic actor. [. . .] As an autistic person, I have thirsted to see individuals from our community represent us in popular culture. We seem to be finally getting a taste of that, thanks to Mickey Rowe. The openly autistic actor will be playing the autistic leading character of 'Curious Incident of the Dog in the Night-Time,' the successful play based on the best-selling book."[1]

You are your own best agent and advocate. No one is going to fight for you and your community the way you will fight for yourself. No one is going to tell you what you deserve or are capable of. You get to tell the world what you are capable of. If you want something done, you have the power to make it happen.

Buoyed by a rushing river of media attention, the time came for me to pack up two suitcases and hop on a flight out to Indiana. At the start of my *Curious Incident* journey I had never traveled completely independently, and now here I was, a confident flyer. I settled into my Indianapolis hotel room, a long-term suite complete with a living room and kitchen. I lay in the crisp sheets of the hotel bed, looked out the window onto the sprawling city, and contemplated the next several months of my existence. I'd be in eight-hour rehearsals six days a week. Christopher is onstage for every moment of the show, meaning I'd be onstage for every moment of those rehearsal days. Meanwhile the other actors might be called to rehearsal less or just in general have more downtime to get to know each other. Then again, free time like that in the rehearsal room is an uncomfortable space for me, and even having time to make friends was a very different beast than knowing how to make a friend when the time came. While you are actively rehearsing you know the words that you are going to say and what other people are going to say in response. Life is predictable. Everyone in the room, yourself included, has a specific role to play. Whether it is another character in the play, director, or stage manager, you know what everyone's role is. But when a break time is called you instantly feel less comfortable. You don't have a specific role during a break time, which makes it confusing for someone on the spectrum. My past experiences in theatre had been profoundly isolating and marked by bullying, and I wondered how this experience would be. I knew that any social isolation would be intensified by the constant physical isolation of being in an unfamiliar city and unable to drive a car.

That said, I was grateful for a break from my home life. Perhaps a few months apart would be a great reset opportunity for my marriage, and a chance for my wife to forge some new bonds with her autistic son, without me around to help bridge the gap. I wondered what developmental milestones new baby brother "F" would pass while I was gone. But I reminded myself that this was financially a great step forward for my young family, especially if these press opportunities continued. My plan was still to make a long-term platform from this opportunity, perhaps speaking engagements and consulting opportunities. My wife still couldn't hold down employment, and I had been limited to menial jobs. *Curious Incident* could change our entire lives. Settled in that knowledge, I fell asleep, knowing I'd need rest before I became immersed in the first day of rehearsal.

On the first day of rehearsal it was just me, the director, the choreographer, and a few stage managers. And an empty chair center stage. Within hours the director and the stage managers had stepped out of the room to leave the choreographer and me to explore how we could make a person float in zero gravity onstage, with no wires, no strings, just a chair. After fifteen minutes of exploration, I made contact with the chair. My abs were pressed against the back top rail of the chair. I leaned forward, shifting my weight in front of me like a blast off ignition sequence, and I flew.

Within days this bliss would be changed as the rest of the cast and dozens more people arrived in the city.

Thankfully, rehearsing *Curious Incident* was the most enjoyable rehearsal process I'd ever been a part of. I got to relish in the experience of seeing myself master a role that people back in Seattle had cautioned was too difficult for someone who'd never before had a speaking role. They warned me I'd likely have a difficult time memorizing such large swaths of script, but they didn't understand that autistics use scripts every day. We use scripting for daily situations that we can predict the outcome of, and we stick to those scripts. My job as an autistic in daily interactions is to make you believe that I am coming up with words on the spot, that this is a spontaneous interaction and the first time the conversation has ever happened in my life. For instance, at a Starbucks coffee shop I often say:

Me: Hi, how are you doing today? (Smile.) Can I please have a tall coffee? Thank you so much! (If it seems like more conversation is needed) Has it been busy today?

Barista: (Any barista response.)

Me: Oh yeah? Is it nicer when it's busy or when it's slow?

Barista: (Any barista response.)

Me: Definitely. Have a great rest of your day!

This is also my job onstage as an actor reciting a monologue from Shakespeare's *King Lear*:

> Wherefore should I
> Stand in the plague of customs, and permit
> The curiosity of nations to deprive me . . .
> When my dimensions are as well compact,
> My mind as generous, and my shape as true . . . ?

It's really no different. They're lines I've learned and say often, but I'm making you believe they are mine and particular to this specific moment. That I'm coming up with the words on the spot.

People often say it must be hard to be a really great actor in spite of my autism, but I am not a great actor in spite of my autism. I am who I am because of my differences. I have had to be an actor my whole life to pass as neurotypical, so being an actor comes so naturally to me.

Christopher does a lot of stimming in the show, the hand-flapping, rocking, spinning movements autistic people sometimes do, and the director and I worked together to take the stims I did naturally and modify them. This made it so they could read more easily on the stage, to be used as devices with which to take or give focus, and even be used as buttons on the end of comedic lines to subconsciously cue the audience when to laugh. My biggest frustration in college was that I really didn't receive much of an acting education. No matter what class I was in, voice class, Shakespeare, scene study, Alexander technique, Stanislavski, or Chekhov, the only notes I would get would be to lose the tension in my hands. The idea of an actor working from a "neutral" body is steeped in ableism. But again, our society is built on ableism, so I spent all four years of college working to get rid of the tension in my hands. I was told if I couldn't get rid of the obvious tension in my hands I would never be cast in a show. So I worked very hard; eventually, with a lot of thought and effort I was able to mask my autism. I was able to hide it. But in *Curious Incident* I got to forget all about that and let that tension come back in a really easy, comfortable way. I got to be myself.

I spent my rehearsal days working with my fellow actors to tumble and climb all around the room, and they were excited to get to know me and learn about autism. Everyone was there to tell a story about autism, and they were all aware of the huge amount of press excitement over this show because of me. That said, I was never made to feel like a freak show their careers were benefiting from. It was a strange delight to be in a work and social environment where everyone knew and loved the fact that I was autistic. I was warmly included in gatherings and outings, and the people who played my parents onstage loved me offstage in a vibrant, constant way that I hadn't known in my real-life parents. To this day, I count some of the people in that cast as some of my dearest friends. Our gatherings outside of rehearsal were some of the most life-giving interactions I'd had in my whole life. Interestingly enough, when my wife came out to visit, these people already knew and loved me enough to confide in me that they thought she was just not good for me and that she wasn't healthy for me. I knew they weren't wrong, but I still clung to hope that maybe this opportunity would set our lives and marriage on a new and positive trajectory. I had made lifelong promises, and if that meant enduring some mistreatment along the way, then okay. For better or for worse. That's what I had agreed to, scratched and sunburned, just a few years earlier.

The show opened and it was incredible! The crowd absolutely went wild as I unicycled out onto the stage. Taking my first bow before a packed house on their feet for me, my heart burst with the knowledge that what I had known about myself had been proved true. I am a great actor, and that is because of, not in spite of my autism. My differences are my strengths. Just like Wolfgang Mozart, Albert Einstein, Greta Thunberg, and Temple Grandin, autistic people like me can excel in and revolutionize their fields. Society may believe that there are so many reasons why I should never be an actor. But acting is a dichotomy: a tension between what is safe and what is dangerous. What is known and what is unknown. What's mundane and what's exciting. I put my dichotomies to work for me. Being a good actor is about doing the work and being in control so the audience trusts you to lead them, and then being vulnerable and letting the audience see your soul. The skill, study, and training help create the trust. The challenges make the vulnerability. You need both of them. As an autistic I have felt vulnerable my entire life. To be vulnerable onstage is no biggie. Being in front of an audience of five hundred or five thousand people is very easy for me. The roles are incredibly clear, logical, and laid out. I am onstage; you are sitting in the seats watching me. I am playing a character, and that is what you want, expect, and are paying for. The conversations onstage are scripted and written much better than the ones in my real life. On the street is where conversations are scary—those roles aren't clear.

Onstage there are often bright lights shining on you, and loud noises that come out of nowhere, "sound cues," but you've rehearsed all these things in advance and you know where each sound cue is happening because it happens in the exact same place every night, so it almost feels like you are in control of those things and because you know what to expect, you are in on the magic.

When I got to play Christopher Boone onstage every night, I got to show all the business leaders who saw the show that they can hire us, that we can do professional work at the highest level, that we get the job done, and that they have no reason to discriminate against developmental disabilities.

There is something about *you* that makes *you* different. You have the power to change the world. Whether you are autistic or not, you have some lived experience that makes you unique from your neighbor, from your friend, from your colleague. This thing that makes you different is why the world needs you. Whether you are indigenous, a single mother immigrant of color, have been housing insecure, grew up on a rural farm, a refugee, or in the South Side of Chicago, there is something about you that is unique. The world needs you not in spite of these things that make you unique, but because of them. Our differences are our greatest strengths.

The press storm continued, now with a flurry of rave reviews.

"A mesmerizing and flawless performance. [. . .] Rowe's portrayal of Christopher almost immediately has the audience eating out of his hand."

"Rowe masterfully brought a treasure trove of emotions—joy, sorrow, pressure, humor, wit, and curiosity—and even athleticism."

"Rowe's vocal tone and physical grace in representing Christopher's vexed self-assurance and awkwardness seemed magical."

During the run of the show my phone was always skittering at my dressing room station, buzzed by notifications popping up like Whack-a-Moles. I had begun receiving Facebook messages and emails every day from autistic people who would never even get the chance to see the play I was in but who said that just knowing that a theatre had cared enough to cast the show in this way changed their lives. People emailed just to share their stories with me. They were people who wanted to be seen, understood, and heard just the way I had felt seen at SCT decades earlier. It was such humbling joy to know that putting myself out there and courageously pursuing my dreams had given others that same courage. I was amazed to know that I could be the kind of support to people that I could only wished to have had at an earlier stage in my life.

There is a story of a beach filled with thousands of stranded starfish as far as the eye can see after a storm had washed them ashore the night before and a small child methodically throwing the starfish back into the water one by one so they wouldn't dry out in the sun. When a passing adult told the child that their efforts didn't matter, as they'd never be able to rescue all the starfish, the child methodically threw in another starfish and yelled back, "It mattered to that one." I was here to make a more equitable world for at least one starfish, my autistic son "A," and it was heartening to know I was throwing plenty more starfish into the ocean where they belonged too.

People want so desperately to fit in that they forget what makes them stand out. Be loud. Take up space. Your contributions and thoughts are as valuable as anyone else's, regardless of what society leads you to believe. The world needs us to follow our dreams not just for our own happiness and fulfillment, but because us walking out our unique dreams is what the world needs. You walking out your dream is a blessing to more people than just yourself. The world needs you more than you know. Don't let your lack of bravery or imagination short the world.

Success isn't about the size of your stage but what you do with it. Success is about how you choose to help each person you can with what you have now. Every day you change someone's life without ever even knowing it. Be you. Exactly who you are. Make noise. Take up space. You will never know the change you make. Butterflies will keep flapping their wings and causing hurricanes. So, trust your gut. Trust your morals. If you didn't exist with all your "imperfections," the world would not be so beautiful. You have got this. You don't even know the ways in which you have made so many people's lives better.

Of my time in Indiana, the acting was the easy part! The hard part was living on my own. Autistic people often have a lot of trouble with executive function, which refers to the mental skills required for ease of navigation through modern daily life, such as flexible thinking. Now, during the show all the actors lived in hotels. We had a company car to share, and I would tag along with others on our weekly trip to the grocery store on Mondays, our one day off each week. Because I couldn't drive myself, I had no way to go back to the store again later in the week if I ran out of food before Monday. So I set a goal for myself every Monday trip: get one week's worth of groceries. And off I would go with my cast, silently repeating my goal like a mantra. "Get one week's worth of groceries, get one week's worth of groceries." Every time I would leave with maybe three apples, a box of Oreos, and a frozen dinner. Needless to say, this is not one week's worth of groceries. My daily Starbucks breakfast sandwiches kept me afloat. Acting is easy. Doing the job is easy. It's the other stuff that is hard. But nonautistic people don't realize that. They often think an autistic person could never be a great actor, because we are too much like robots to convey powerful emotions onstage. This stems from the common and damaging misconception that people on the spectrum either don't feel emotion or don't have emotion. That's simply not true. We feel emotions just like anyone else and can identify them within ourselves. What's hard for us is correctly reading other people's emotions, unless they're being really clear. In real life, I'll often think someone's really, really mad at me, when they aren't at all. Or someone could be really, really mad at me, and I don't pick up on that. That doesn't mean that I don't feel angry myself ever, or understand what the emotion anger is. It just means that I can't always identify that in other people. But in the context of a play, I'm able to read the script as many times as I want and I can analyze everything that happens before I get in the rehearsal room. At that point, we all sit down and talk about what's happening in each scene before we even begin acting it out. In that situation, I'm not the only one trying to understand the social interaction! *Everyone* in the room around the table is trying to under-stand the social interaction! All that to say, it's so ironic to me that nonautis-tic people are quick to discourage autistic people from acting because they think we can't do it, but meanwhile they expect us to be able to function easily in normal life. They've got the situation completely backward!

The run in Indiana was coming to a close, and it was nearly time for me to head back to Seattle for two days before moving on to New York. The press storm was still roaring, and it got to a point where I had made the news nearly everywhere one could make the news. Only one major publication was missing, and I was determined. I had made many attempts to explain to the *New York Times* why the casting of a disabled actor in a disabled role was important, but for months my emails had gone unanswered, swallowed up into a black hole. One of the strengths of autistic people is an ability to look at things in out-of-the-box ways, and I chose to focus on the fact that although I hadn't received a response, that also meant that they hadn't said they were not interested either. Always ask for what you want. Always try. Make the other person say no to you, instead of you saying no to yourself before they even get a chance to say no to you. So I still had a chance. I couldn't get the gatekeeper to care, so I decided I'd go over the gate. I threw myself into research with the same determination with which I'd researched how to get in touch with the Broadway casting team. I bought a one-month subscription to the *New York Times*, just long enough for me to look up everyone who had ever written for the *NYT* theatre section. Then I started narrowing down my list based on the writers who seemed to have some understanding of diversity and inclusion. I knew that this didn't mean they would necessarily understand disability or feel that disability needed to be included, but it was still the best path forward that I could see. Then I took to Twitter, tweeting these writers an article about my show and explaining to them why this was important and why it was more than just a play. I asked them what their barriers to covering the show might be and how I could help remove those barriers.

It felt like another long shot in the dark, just like emailing the Lincoln Center box office. But once again, the long shot found its target. While sitting in Seattle's Sea-Tac Airport, waiting for my flight to Syracuse, my Twitter app pinged. I was thrilled to see that one of the *NYT* theatre writers had finally tweeted me back, albeit with some clearly generic response. Nev-ertheless, I seized the opportunity and tweeted back with more information about why my casting was so important. I heard nothing more and focused on getting settled in Syracuse. Then, on the first day of tech rehearsals, Syracuse Stage leadership let me know that an unbelievably unusual thing had happened. An *NYT* theatre writer had let them know they were coming out to Syracuse to interview me and review the show. They couldn't believe it! Only the local paper had ever been interested in covering their productions, and because of that they only ever reached out to the local paper. I couldn't believe that I'd actually made it happen. It was true. You are your own best agent, and no one is going to fight for you or your dreams the way you will fight for yourself. When we work on one stone at a time, we can move mountains. I was going to be interviewed in the *New York Times*!

The writer and I had made plans to meet at a coffee shop across the street from the theatre, early in the morning before my matinee. I arrived even before the shop had opened for the day. I nervously stuffed a large handful of mints into my mouth, so I could have fresh breath for my big interview. Unfortunately, at that exact same moment the writer arrived. I shook her hand and garbled all the initial pleasantries with a mouth filled and fizzing with dissolving mints! I'd hazard a guess that she wondered at first if that's just the way autism made me speak, giving her dire concerns about the quality of the performance she was there to review. We ducked in from the drizzly chill just as a barista unlocked the door. I eventually managed to chomp down the mints, and we dove into the meat of the interview.

Although I was terrified, that also meant that I was pushing myself and growing. I try to always find the fear in the room and face it. For an autistic person, spontaneous conversations with people can be scary. Formal interviews are usually less scary than interactions on the street, because there are the really clear roles of interviewer and interviewee. The interviewer asks the questions and I, the interviewee, am supposed to sound smart; those are the roles. And I can prepare ahead of time with some scripting of what I'd like to say. But during this particular interview, whenever I looked at my scripted notes the reporter stopped me. "No, I want to hear what *you* have to say. What you think. Not what's written on these papers." I tried to explain that what I had written on the papers was what I thought, it was what I had to say. That is why I had taken the time to write it down the day before. The intense nervousness crept back in. I don't think she knew how steeped in ableism her request was. I usually bring pages of notes to interviews, so I can refer to them as needed instead of completely making things up as I go. It is a really helpful tool to help me get by in a society that is difficult for autistic people to navigate, and it doesn't hurt anyone else in any way. Asking an autistic person to go without their scripts should be considered as unreasonable as asking someone who uses hearing aids to go without them, or someone who uses a wheelchair to go without. But ableism is the water the fish swim in, and people just don't realize how entrenched it is in them.

The interview ended up lasting a whole two hours, continuing until the artistic director of the theatre had to walk across the street to the coffee shop and inform the journalist that my matinee was starting soon and that I needed to have time to at least get my costume on and get a few minutes of stretching and vocal warm-ups in. Phew. I had made it through the big interview, and in the final published piece she did mention that I referred to notes and why that was. I hope this means she learned something about autism during our time talking together in that coffee shop. The interview was eventually published as an *NYT* article, as well as a glossy six-page article in *NYT Magazine*. I love this one quote from the *NYT* article:

"Mr. Rowe plays Christopher with an agile grace, an impish humor and a humanizing restraint. On Broadway, where the play was a Tony Award–winning hit, it ran eight times a week, with two actors alternating the demanding role of Christopher, a 15-year-old with autism who sets out to solve a mystery. Mr. Rowe—thought to be the first openly autistic actor to play the role—does all nine shows a week."

11

Our deepest fear is not that we are inadequate. Our deepest fear is that we are powerful beyond measure. It is our light, not our darkness, that most frightens us. We ask ourselves, who am I to be brilliant, gorgeous, talented, and fabulous? Actually, who are you not to be? You are a child of God. Your playing small doesn't serve the world. There's nothing enlightened about shrinking so that other people won't feel insecure around you. We are all meant to shine, as children do. We are born to make manifest the glory of God that is within us. It's not just in some of us, it's in everyone. And as we let our own light shine, we unconsciously give other people permission to do the same. As we are liberated from our own fear, our presence automatically liberates others.

—Marianne Williamson

Curious Incident closed, the press attention finally let up a little, and I flew home feeling buoyant. The knowledge that I was now a well-known actor with a stellar credit on my resume and a host of rave reviews splashed with my name made me feel like I was soaring at heights well beyond my seat on the plane. I was excited for where my career would go next and hopeful that this would all lead to a peaceful home life.

Back in Seattle, nobody would audition me. They were still scared to talk to an actually autistic person. Even though I'd received national press and acclaim, I was back to being unable to get work or auditions. Perhaps that's the risk I took by my breakout role being an autistic role. Now people thought that all I could do was play autistic characters.

Nothing changed for the better in my marriage either. Standing with my luggage in the doorway to my home, all thoughts of the grime of a long flight were washed away as two sets of little feet eagerly toddled toward me. I dropped to their level and showered them with warm hugs, nuzzles that made them burst into giggles, and brightly pitched words of love, all to assure them of how much I had missed them. I toppled out my apartment door into the hallway outside, their toddler weight falling on top of me, still tightly hugging me and giggling. Still not fully inside my home yet, having been stopped by little ones needing loving on, I picked one up in each arm and stood up to look for my wife. My eyes landed on Grey's icy glare, and she immediately launched into a tirade about some perceived slight from months earlier.

Grey was a teetering wineglass perched right on the edge of a table. And I was standing in the doorway, nearly frozen, just waiting for the inevitable crash.

Living with abuse is an all too familiar reality for many developmentally disabled people. The rate of violent victimization among disabled people is more than two times that of nondisabled people. Among those crime victims with disabilities, the rate of violent victimization of people with cognitive disabilities is more than two times higher again. I'd grown up and moved out to escape a traumatic childhood home life, only to quickly find myself trapped in a marriage to a new abuser. I several times ended up calling the police when my wife was inflicting domestic violence on me. Unfortunately, sometimes police think that there is no way a woman could be violently abusive toward a man. They sometimes think that this would mean the real issue was with the man's lack of masculinity and not his partner who was violently controlling him. When I called the police, upon arriving, they would realize that the person who called them for help was not a woman as they had likely first assumed, but a man. Then they would leave.

Obviously if you put a frog into a pot of boiling water, the frog will just say, "Oh heck no!" and jump out. But if you put a frog into a pot of slightly hot water and then bring the water up to a boil, the frog will accept everything as normal and cook to death. This was my relationship with Grey.

I came to accept that I wasn't making progress as an actor in Seattle, so undeterred I decided to go to grad school to study leadership instead. I was determined to make forward motion, even if that meant existing in a leadership capacity instead of as a performer. As painful as it was to accept that acting might not happen again, perhaps this was a blessing in disguise. Perhaps this was all meant to lead me to a brilliant next step to take toward my goal of changing the industry, seeing as I'd already done all I could to break new ground as an actor. I began a course at grad school, and I suppose all my years of juggling came into play as I kept a precarious rotation of early morning opening shifts, late night student life, and round-the-clock parenthood. Years of street performing had made me a seasoned professional at keeping all the balls in the air even when being heckled by strangers passing by, but it's a little more difficult to keep it all going when you have to live with your heckler. While boiling water for coffee one morning thinking I was alone in the kitchen, I suddenly heard Grey's tight, penetrating voice around the corner threatening to cut up my suits and clothes unless I stopped attending grad school immediately. While at school and trying my best to focus on lectures, I would receive text messages letting me know that if I was not home in ten minutes, one piece of property or another would be destroyed. On other days, even days of exams, she texted me to come home immediately from class or "something bad would happen." I ended up dropping out of school, hoping that would end the abuse.

Most nights Grey would go out to bars and not come home until 6:00 or 7:00 a.m. I don't know what she could have been doing out on the town that long for so many nights a week. I would get bored staying at a bar every night until 7:00 a.m. I was mostly upset because the grad school that I had received a scholarship for seemed much more valuable for our family.

When I was growing up, my grandpa, my mother, and even my classmates had frequently told me that I would be lucky if I found anyone who wanted to marry me, so I was ready and willing to put up with a lot to make a marriage work! I knew that autistic people and people with developmental disabilities were not traditionally seen as sexy. So, I tried my best to be okay with whatever came my way! But over time the target of physical abuse moved from me to my children, and I knew I had to get out. I was strong enough to put up with abuse. I could make that choice. My children, however, did not make that choice. I believe that having a mental illness is never a person's fault, but it is not the fault of their children either.

I pushed up my glasses, which were constantly at the bottom of my nose, having slowly slid down under their own weight like a melting glacier down the side of a mountain.

The whole next year I felt like my stomach had been permanently twisted into one of my clown balloon creations, like a poodle, or a giraffe. The twisted connections between the legs and necks of the animals felt tight in my stomach. Sometimes when I get overwhelmed, I try not to think about emotions because after everything else I simply do not have the energy for them. Sometimes I try to just focus on the facts. The tangibles. Lists are good. Lists tend to bring order to situations that feel like they have none. Lists tends to calm the chaos. I'm sorry, dear reader, if this is not how your brain works. But this is sometimes how my brain works. And this is my book. And you are reading it.

Grey might have a different book, and I respect that her situation was and still is very different than mine.

So, here is a list of the things that happened that next year:

- My younger son turned two years old. He nearly always had patches of skin that had been scratched or picked off from his face by Grey.
- Both he and my older son would frequently tell me that it was Grey who was picking the skin off my younger son's face.
- As "A" and "F" got older and older, they also became more articulate and their descriptions of Grey's physical harm to them became more and more detailed.
- I felt overwhelmed. I felt confused.
- For the first time in my life I felt depressed knowing that my own children were suffering because of a choice I made. Because of who I chose to marry. I reached out for help everywhere I could find it.
- I myself, my children's pediatrician, and the children's hospital all called child protective services for help. When the child protective services social worker heard I had autism, though, she told me that I had better be careful contacting them for help because with my autism diagnosis if they found that the children were being injured by Grey they would likely need to take the children from both of us.
- This confused me because I was not the one injuring the children. I was the one begging for someone to make the injuries to my younger child stop.
- It was so embarrassing that the social worker told me she would not be able to help me to keep my children safe because of my autism. I realize that the Department of Children, Youth and Families is morbidly overworked, understaffed, and underfunded. But when you have such an important job, and so much power, don't you have a responsibility to do the work? To be creative?
- I was a foolish mortal as someone once said.

- I had text messages from Grey to myself telling me how sorry she was that she hurt the children. I had pictures of "F" taken both by myself and his doctors.
- Grey, who had been diagnosed with psychosis, checked herself into Fairfax Hospital, a mental health hospital that she had been to before, and for the first time in years I felt calm and safe. I felt hope that this could be the solution. That soon this would all be better. I breathed a breath of fresh air.
- An incessant vibrating in my stomach and chest had stopped for the first time in years.
- Unfortunately, when Grey returned things were only worse.
- Grey told me she was having "visual and auditory hallucinations," which I believe means she was hearing voices. I remember this because she told me both in text message writing and verbally.
- I found "F" with a large, quarter-size circle of skin missing all the way down to the muscle right by his nose under his eye.
- Grey told me verbally and in writing that her fingernail had been the culprit that caused the injury.
- The knots in my stomach instantly returned.
- Grey told me that the world was growing colder and darker and that she was scared.
- Grey told me and her therapist that she was planning on killing my mother. I recorded this conversation on my cell phone as I didn't know what else to do. I needed a witness, someone to see what was happening in our house.
- Grey went out with her best friend Janet to dance, get drinks, and help Grey chase the darkness away. They both came home at 5:00 a.m. I know this because I waited up for her.
- The next day Janet texted me. She told me that I need to take my two little ones and get out of the house. I don't know what Grey had told Janet the night before to make her say that, but I knew I needed to act.
- My stomach was sick. I was so mad at Grey. So confused.
- I was so mad at Grey, but at the same time, Grey's mental health was a disability. This was not Grey's fault. But this was also not my children's fault.
- My older son had a therapist named Paula who had been hired to help Grey navigate his autism. I called her many times asking her for guidance and advice.

- I didn't think I was necessarily religious, but I called any religious leader I could think of, asking them for guidance.
- Grey took "F" to the children's hospital with a second injury, and while he was in the hospital they photographed it. His eye was nearly swollen shut just on the opposite side of his nose to where the pick mark had been before.
- This was nauseating to me. I did not know how to make this sit with my view of disability. Surely Grey's mental health counted as a disability.
- I was overwhelmed. I needed someone to tell me what to do in this situation. What was the way a person is supposed to respond to this? I didn't know. I was just myself. No character. No role to play. Just myself in a gale force wind at sea.

No. Wait. Stop.

I did have a role. I did have a character. I was dad to my two-year-old and three-year-old. I was a papa bear. Even though many people had told me to get out, it still felt like the hardest decision of my life. To take children away from their mother is a really big deal. But I was a father. That was my role. And while Grey's mental health was in no way her fault, this was also definitely not the fault of "A" and "F."

Mother's Day was two days away. And no matter what, I couldn't take the children when Mother's Day was so near. So I stayed home 24/7, babysitting Grey while she babysat the children over the next two days and then made sure that Grey had the best Mother's Day I could possibly give her.

The next day before Grey woke up, I was gone. With the car seats and the children. And just as many of their things as I could fit in the back of a car. I went straight to the courthouse and presented all the text messages. From Grey. From her friend Janet telling me to get out. Photos of the injuries.

I should have acted sooner.

- By the end of the year, the court put restraining orders on Grey three times, protecting me and the little ones from her, and denied each of her motions to change its decisions.
- The children and I spent the whole next year going to an office building, this time set up like an apartment with everything except for a bedroom, so that Grey could visit the children for a few hours while a professional supervisor watched them.

- The other problem making me feel like I was going to throw up seasick from this storm was that someone needed to pay these social workers and pay for this office that looked like a little apartment, and that someone was me. It was costing me close to $1,000 per week, and that is money I simply did not have. That was more than I could ever imagine spending on rent. I simply assumed once the court decided the children needed to be kept safe, that the children would be kept safe. I didn't think they would only be kept safe if I could afford to pay for this professional supervision. I needed another solution. While it was important to keep my baby bears physically safe and well, it was also important to keep them financially safe and well.
- To end these costs, my lawyer and I came up with a parenting plan where Grey could see the children unsupervised again but only if Grey provided monthly compliance reports from her psychiatrist and psychologist, them signing off every month giving her the okay. This way the children would be a motivation for Grey to get help. She could work toward seeing the children again unsupervised, and the children would be the reward for her staying on top of her mental health. It would help everyone and hopefully keep the children from continuing to get hurt. Grey would not accept this and decided to stay in professionally supervised visitations.
- The court and I hired a parenting evaluator to look at the parenting plan I had created, where Grey could see the children again unsupervised if she provided monthly compliance reports from her providers, and if she didn't provide a monthly compliance report we would go back to visiting her with a supervisor. After two years of Grey choosing not to sign this new parenting plan—after two long years—she finally decided to sign it. And this is what we have now.
- It's not perfect, but nothing in life is. It was as good as I had the energy to do. And I had grace for that.
- I breathed a slight sigh of relief. Though this experience had put a dent in my hull that I couldn't remove.
- People sometimes ask me if I think that all the hard things in life happened to me for a reason. If all the good things happened for a reason too. Or is everything in life just random? I don't know. But I do believe that we can make choices. And through our choices we can create the meaning. We can make the hardest parts of our life worth it. We can find and create the meaning by using our lived experiences to make

things better for the next generations. The choices we make create the meaning every day. In love. In life. In friendship.

I was now a single dad who could not drive a car, often with full custody of my two children. No matter how hard being a single dad was, I was lucky. Because many people with developmental disabilities like autism can't have kids. Society prefers to infantilize disabled people and imagine that we never have sex, perhaps either disgusted by the idea of our bodies experiencing pleasure or hoping that if we don't reproduce, our kind will finally go away. It's still brazenly legal and relatively straightforward and easy for any parent to have their developmentally disabled child sterilized.

I believe this is because of the Supreme Court case *Buck v. Bell*, which passed 8–1, stating, "It is legal for a state to forcibly sterilize its own citizens who are deemed unfit." This law was created specifically for people with disabilities, referring to them as the "feeble minded." This law has never been overturned.

When lawyer Mark Bold came across this 1920s law that allowed for the forced sterilization of people with disabilities, he was shocked. Surely this wasn't still happening today. So he decided to call his county clerk's office pretending that he had a disabled daughter, just to see what would happen. He wanted to see if this was still happening, if this was possible, how difficult it was. And he recorded his call:

WOMAN: County Clerk's office.

MARK BOLD: Yes, is [beep] there please?

WOMAN: She's on the phone, do you want to hold?

MARK BOLD: Yeah, that'd be great. Thank you.

WOMAN: [beep] speaking.

MARK BOLD: Hey, this is Mark. I talked to you earlier this morning here when I was driving. You called and you told me to call you back if I had any questions or what have you. It is in regards to my handicapped daughter and the sterilization.

WOMAN: Yes, yes.

MARK BOLD: Okay. So I now have the chance to obviously sit down at the desk here. I took some time off work and wanted to find out what steps—

WOMAN: You're gonna do a motion for sterilization. And you're gonna tell the judge the reason why you need that done and, you know, the situation. And then it'll come to me. I'll set a hearing. You guys will have a hearing on it. And the judge will make the decision which more—most of the times, you know, they know that this needs to be done. So I don't think that you're gonna have a problem, you know?

MARK BOLD: Okay.

WOMAN: And then we'll set a hearing. As soon as I get it, I'll get it to [beep] and she'll give you a call.

MARK BOLD: I'll just write a letter. Is that what I need to do?

WOMAN: You're gonna do a motion handwrite your daughter's name, then under that motion for—and then write out what you need.

MARK BOLD: Okay. So I'll say motion . . .

WOMAN: And then you put your number on the bottom where we can reach you.

MARK BOLD: Okay. This is not a—we're not gonna be the first one to do this. Okay, to us, we feel weird about it, you know what I mean? I mean, it's just . . .

WOMAN: No absolutely not. Oh no, sir. You're absolutely not the first ones. A lot of—this has to be done, because we have so many problems with—yeah, you have to do this. It's for her best.

MARK BOLD: Exactly. I don't think people understand this type—you know, these type of people, they're difficult.

WOMAN: No. You are—no, no you are doing the best thing. The problem is, is when we get some that don't do it and then it's a problem, you know, that has to be dealt with. But no sir, you are doing what you're supposed to.

MARK BOLD: Okay.

WOMAN: You just send it straight to me, and I'll get every—pull the file and get everything taken care of.

MARK BOLD: Okay. All right. Well, thank you so much.

WOMAN: Okay, you're welcome.

MARK BOLD: All right. Bye bye.[1]

So many people with developmental disabilities alive today, like Anna Seal, for example, have been sterilized, so I was privileged to get to be a single dad.

For Anna Seal, it was determined that she was "feeble minded" and "retarded" and she was forced to live in a home, the Central Virginia Training Center, which was closed just this year. Today Anna lives in a two-bedroom apartment full of plants and with two pet birds. Because she was able to live so independently, she was eventually told she could leave the center if she would just agree to be sterilized. She said no. She had always wanted to have kids. And besides, her job at the center was even to take care of the children who lived there. When she was nineteen years old, two nurses came into her room and told her she was going to get a standard checkup. They put an anesthesia mask on her and she passed out. When she woke up, she had a scar and had been sterilized against her will. These laws were created during the eugenics push in 1920s. But they are still used frequently today. A misguided attempt toward Darwinism.[2]

Speaking of Darwin, there is an evolutionary theory that suggests that autism is not a genetic flaw. Rather, it is an evolutionary advantage. A tribe that has someone who can think outside the box and create new ways of doing things is more likely to flourish and advance as a society. A caveman who is less interested in chattering with others and instead more interested in hitting rocks together is the one more likely to make a spark of fire. The herder who can remember in great detail the health and lineage of each animal in their flock is more likely to breed strong and healthy livestock. In today's hypersocial society, an ability to intuitively form social connections is most valued. But for much of human history, it was perhaps the hunter who didn't spend much time with others but instead came up with new and more efficient ways of hunting who was the most valuable member of their community. Even the most desirable for reproduction.

This autism gain is not relegated to hunter-gatherer communities of the ancient past. In more recent history, Mozart, Einstein, and Michelangelo have all been suspected by historians to have been autistic. A quick glance throughout even contemporary leaders and visionaries in respective fields shows people with autism are still leading the way. Greta Thunberg, the teenage climate change activist. Temple Grandin, who is the nation's most expert designer of humane facilities for livestock.

What about your lived experience makes you different? What is your superpower?

Darwin said the one thing, the one incredible ingredient, to which we all owe our existence on earth is variation. That is the secret sauce, Darwin says. The magic. Variation is what makes for perfection.

So, I was a single dad and no matter how hard it was, I was so grateful.

Disabled people are not inherently worse at being parents simply because of our disabilities. Sometimes society might make it so some aspects of our parenting journey are harder or have to look a little different, but that's a different thing entirely than us being worse parents. And while there are barriers to us parenting in all the same ways as everyone else, there are also so many moments where our differences are our strengths. In my case, I was a single father with full custody, but due to my eyesight I had no ability to drive. I had to cobble together rides from my family and burn money on Lyfts and taxis in order to get my children to supervised visitations three times per week so that their mother could play with them. I also found that when other adults at day cares and playgrounds see the autistic man with headphones on rocking or flapping, they don't know what to make of you. "He's surely not the father," they think. "I suppose he is a really interesting choice for a nanny," they likely think as they scooch themselves and their kids away from me. Worse still would be when total strangers would ask my kids if they were okay, and if they knew who I was. Again, none of this meant that I was a lesser parent due to my disability, but it was the perception of an ableist society that is not used to seeing disabled people in public, let alone seeing them parenting in public. By reading this book and spreading these words, you are doing so much to make the world a better place and work toward disability acceptance and disability inclusion.

Within my family, we see the ways in which my autism is a win for us. It's been so lovely for me to see the bond I have with my autistic son "A," and how I'm able to be a support for him. For example, when sometimes he regulates himself with stims that might cause him injury, I understand what's going on and why, and I am able to casually suggest some other, gentler stims he can try instead.

I often find it helpful to say and demonstrate it like, "Hey buddy, you might hurt yourself. When I feel like doing that, I sometimes try rubbing my fingers together, or tapping on my leg." I think it's really powerful that I am able to normalize stimming for him in that way, while also redirecting him to things that are more gentle on his body, that also might pass more easily for neurotypical. (Because just being yourself is always best, but sometimes being able to pass as neurotypical is just sadly easier.) If a nonautistic parent saw an autistic child stimming, they might simply tell the child to stop, but this isn't helpful since the autistic child is stimming to self-regulate! It's a coping mechanism that helps them and shouldn't be taken away. It's just fine, however, to work with them to figure out something else that will be helpful for them. I also think I am equipped to be an excellent advocate for my kid when interacting with teachers, medical professionals, or even other parents and their kids. There is so much misunderstanding surrounding autism, and one of the ways I am able to make the world a more equitable place for my son is by being able to explain his needs and behaviors while he doesn't yet have the vocabulary to do so. I enjoy being able to be an active and knowledgeable participant in education and health care decisions related to his diagnosis. I am so glad that my son has a dad who is well equipped to go to bat for him in that arena. When I peruse a prospective school's glossy pamphlet about how they provide for disabled and special education students, I can read through the lines to know what they actually mean, since I have experienced it all for myself. Autistic adults like myself exist, and so if anyone wants to learn about autism, they don't need to ask the nonautistic parent of a child on the spectrum, or reference theories created without input from the autism community. You can talk to an adult with autism directly. We are the experts on our own lives.

My other son "F" doesn't have an autism diagnosis, and I am still an excellent parent for him as well. My autism has meant that I have had to hone the skills to be a dynamic problem solver in order to make it through society. This translates into me being a parent who is uniquely equipped to help my small children navigate a society that's not set up for them either. There is so much in a child's world that doesn't make sense to them yet, and I am able to have such great empathy in moments where that is feeling especially overwhelming for them. My craving for proprioceptive input means I am so eager to be on the ground tumbling or up high clambering in a tree with my kids. My younger son loves to be swung around or tossed high in the air, and I also enjoy the sensation of swinging him. Long walks by myself while listening to an audiobook have always been a place of solace for me, and both my sons so enjoy going on long stroller journeys with me at that time, especially if I set them up with a few snacks and pinwheels to hold. My childhood obsession with circus arts means if I need to quickly entertain them, I can put on a juggling show with anything from sticks on the ground to fruit in the fruit bowl. Kids love candy, but I promise you that they especially love it if you pull it out of their brother's nose. I can always have them enthralled. There are so many ways in which being autistic gives you a natural inclination to be a really wonderful parent.

Being an autistic parent isn't inherently hard. Being a single parent of young children is hard for anyone, though. Every little thing feels more complicated. I remember one time when my kids and I had finally sat down to eat at a restaurant, when one expressed that he needed to go potty. If you have a partner, such a situation is no big deal. One stays with the food, your things, and the other kid, and the other quickly does the bathroom trip. But when you're a single parent, you have to scoop everyone up and leave enough things at your table to make sure the waitstaff don't clear away your food or think you've dined and dashed, but take anything actually valuable with you. Then you have to facilitate one child using the potty while also keeping the other one from touching everything. You are just alone through everything. If you're sick, there's no one else who can bear the brunt for a day or two while you rest. It's the same deal if you need to take an important phone call or run an errand that would otherwise be quick and easy.

You are also doing everything on a single income. My financial situation became dire, since I now needed to support my children as a single parent and get through a divorce process, but I still couldn't get anyone to agree to give me an audition or a job interview. So I decided to produce my own work. Producing your own work is also called working from home, and you can attempt to do it while being a single dad with no ability to drive.

I produced theatre with a company I founded, Arts on the Waterfront. Though it never paid me a penny, when we did *Romeo and Juliet*, we partnered with the Trevor Project, an LGBTQIA suicide prevention organization for people who feel the need to kill themselves because society doesn't accept who they love. When we did *Waiting for Godot* outside on the streets, we partnered with homeless artists and an organization called Teen Feed that provides safe places for homeless teens.

After that, I founded National Disability Theatre. I grew it from just an idea into a fully fledged nonprofit company working in partnership with Tony Award–winning regional theatres around the country like La Jolla Playhouse and the Goodman Theatre. I grew it into a company that received funding from the Ford Foundation.

In July 2018 I threw out an idea into a Facebook group for disabled theatre artists. The industry was happily wallowing in a rut of either telling the same problematic story about disability again and again or excluding it altogether. At the time disabled actors were only being allowed to play disabled characters, while still 95 percent of disabled characters were being played by nondisabled actors. What if we created a company that was composed exclusively of disabled theatre professionals, and we partnered with all the major regional and Broadway theatre houses to demonstrate that authentic disability representation is powerful, creative, and sexy? A company that would allow disabled artists to play meaty characters even if the biggest struggle in those characters' lives was not disability related. My disabled colleagues expressed their interest and support, so I got to work networking, sending press releases, and being the same tenacious me that had gotten this nobody actor from Seattle in front of Broadway casting directors.

I had long believed that people with disabilities deserve to see successful professionals at the top of their game who will tell them that if you are different, if you access the world differently, then the world needs you! I also wanted to flip the script and eliminate the single story of people with disabilities and show that we are neither inspirational nor charity cases, just powerful and ferocious professionals.

I wanted audiences to see that universal design helps everyone! Not just those with disabilities. We all benefit from universal design every day. Accommodations for people with disabilities are not "charity." Accommodating people with disabilities is not a "burden." As you know, if you are in the airport pulling your luggage and you see stairs and a ramp, you use the ramp! If you are watching a video on public transportation or in the library, or waiting room, you use captions. If you are pushing a stroller and need to cross the street, you use the curb cut. People with disabilities need these accommodations to be included, but this universal design helps make everyone's lives easier. I'll say it again. Just as a reminder. Universal accessible design helps everyone. All of us. So I wanted to use universal design as one of the artistic building blocks for our shows from day one of the design process. But mostly I felt we are at a time in our country where we really need hope, and we really need incredible artistry that could be used as evidence that our differences are our strengths.

Captioning would be artistically integrated into our shows' projection designs. Audio description would be built into a show's sound design for every audience member, making the sound design even more exciting. I was excited for our audience members who didn't have disabilities to experience some of these accommodations. I thought it would help bring them on board in understanding what accessibility is really all about.

Additionally, we would partner with regional theatres and performing arts institutions around the country, which would be mutually beneficial. National Disability Theatre would gain access to those theatres' administrative infrastructure, which would add to our organizational strengths, and our partnering organizations would receive NDT's diversity and programming as well as an education on how to be comfortable working with a whole spectrum of artists and audiences with disabilities. After we left any regional theatre that we partnered with, all these accessibility tools would have been added to that partner organization's tool kit and vocabulary, and they would continue some of those accessibility practices both for their performers and their audiences after we left. We really got to spread the seeds of accessibility all around the country.

In September 2019 I found myself in a rehearsal room belonging to the Tony Award–winning La Jolla Playhouse, surrounded by no one except disabled theatre professionals, all there to workshop National Disability Theatre's first show. It was a history-making moment. Never before in the history of professional American theatre had a show been cast with and created by exclusively disabled professionals. Furthermore, many of the actors had never been in a room before with other disabled people, let alone a rehearsal room. They didn't know any other disabled adults. Ableist society is so incredibly isolating for disabled folx. As I led a movement workshop around the room, many people started crying. They had never before been trusted to move around the room, to fully use their bodies onstage or to fully show their bodies onstage. They had never before been able to move around the room without feeling like everyone was looking at them. Here, everyone was different. No one was looking at them because every person in the room was moving differently.

It went on to be a gorgeous, colorful, moving, magical show about the history of disability rights, touring to schools across Southern California. After seeing our show, three schools immediately enacted structural changes like adding ramps or lifts to their buildings to create accessibility for their disabled students. My heart was so full to know that something I directed led to tangible change in the lives of disabled kids. Disability gain refers to the good that comes from a person's disability: how it has positively affected their personality, worldview, creative problem solving, tenacity, and more. We beautifully showcased disability gain with a Mustang made out of two wheelchairs, and the young audiences were spellbound watching wheelchairs weave and spin around each other in graceful dance. Not only were we all disabled, but we also put onstage the kind of intersectionally diverse casting I've wished to see industry-wide. A trans role was played by a trans actor, who also played a role that would typically be cast with a cisgender woman. The cast was 50 percent POC, and it was a magical moment every time Latinx students would feel comfortable enough to come up postshow to pepper the Spanish-speaking Latinx actor with questions in Spanish. The show's tour was ultimately cut short due to COVID-19, but I'm forever proud of how much it achieved during its short run.

As much as theatre likes to tout itself as being about shared experiences of humanity and enacting social change, by and large I have seen it all be about money. Most professional productions are funded by donors and investors, and they demand to see return on their investment. Getting my industry-changing endeavor off the ground required a lot of money, which I certainly did not have. I would have to secure funding from major donors in order to build NDT beyond an idea or a single production into a fully fledged, sustainable organization.

Imagine you are visiting a very fancy restaurant for the first time, accompanied by someone you're only just getting to know, but you know they are extraordinarily wealthy and interested in getting to know you more. You're clothed in your finest evening wear. The space is expansive and lit dimly by candlelight. The menu is elegant and elaborate, printed in a delicate cursive. The pages are teeming with unfamiliar delicacies. The night begins with small talk as you await your food.

What a glamorous dream, right? Are these a few of your favorite things?

If so, I'm happy for you. They are *not* the favorites of an autistic and legally blind man.

Now, the usual method of securing funding involves a scenario much like I wrote about above, and at this point in the book I'm sure you can figure out why all of that doesn't make for an ideal situation for me. But all of us, autistic or not, have to push through discomfort to achieve our dreams. So I went courageously after mine. NDT's first year of existence was funded by the Ford Foundation after I had written them a letter. The time came to look to the future, and that was going to require a more traditional meeting. I once again found myself crossing the country on a flight to New York City, although this time not to pitch myself for employment in an audition. This time I would be pitching the organization I'd founded, hoping to be able to secure employment for many disabled artists.

Soon my suit and I found ourselves in the restaurant. The head of the foundation looked as though he had just walked off one of New York's avant-garde fashion show runways. I was doing my old familiar play of asking my dinner partner what on the menu was looking good to them. Always stick to the script. This one always did a brilliant job of covering for the fact that my eyes can't decipher the menu. The small talk at this dinner couldn't be scripted, and it was terrifying. Only 10 percent of conversation was spent on the actual work I was doing with National Disability Theatre. Most of the conversation was just about . . . other stuff. Terrifying! But my courage won out, and I left the restaurant with a belly full of filet mignon and a mind reeling with the knowledge that the Ford Foundation had agreed to triple our funding the next year. We had done it!

I had secured funding from major donors like the Ford Foundation. I had received partnerships with theatres such as La Jolla Playhouse and the Goodman Theatre. We had commissioned plays from Pulitzer Prize–nominated disabled artists.

In May 2020 I stepped down as founding artistic director of National Disability Theatre, insisting that I be replaced by a disabled BIPOC artistic director. Sometimes being a great leader requires stepping out of the way. I wonder which world leaders could benefit from learning this lesson.

Leadership is not about power. Leadership is not about popularity. Leadership is about doing what is right. Leadership is about making the moral choice irresistible.

Leadership isn't a position. Leadership is an action.

May 30, 2020

This letter is my official notice that I am resigning from my position of Artistic Director at National Disability Theatre, effective immediately. I wish, however, for this to be made a public announcement at a later date. At this current moment in time the internet's attention is locked on covering the fight for justice and equity for Black people, sparked by the murders of George Floyd, Breonna Taylor, Ahmaud Arbery and a grievously enormous number of others. The disability community grieves in solidarity knowing that between 33 and 50% of all people killed by police are disabled and that Black disabled folx have a 55% chance of being arrested by the age of 28. Therefore, I do not think it wise nor good allyship to take this moment to draw attention to a leader in the disability community simply stepping down from his position. I leave it to NDT's remaining leadership to decide in consultation with the Black community as to when might be a more judicious time to break the news.

NDT will forever be one of my proudest achievements and brought me some of the greatest joys. I am so proud of the work we did to ensure that our revolution was intersectional and lifted other historically oppressed minority groups along with us. I could not be more pleased with our 2019 artist employment statistics, which included the following paying contracts:

94% (17/18) identified as disabled or "it's complicated."
55% (10/18) were non-male.
50% (4/8) of actor contracts went to Black, indigenous, or people of color.
100% (8/8) of the creative team members (designers, directors, and writers) identified as disabled.
27% (5/18) of all individuals identified as LGBTQIA.
100% (8/8) of actor contracts were professional Actors' Equity Association Union contracts.

This achievement was no easy feat, and it required tenacity and my unwavering insistence that we would not compromise on any of these points. Many theatre companies claim to value equity, diversity and inclusion but have yet to attain such statistics, claiming it is too difficult, unrealistic or impossible to achieve. I am forever proud of the work I did to show that it is indeed possible. I wonder which other theatre companies in the nation had diversity statistics comparable to mine at NDT's. I would love to be notified if any did, as that would refresh my hope in the industry. I at least want to be notified if any theatre companies, past or present, ever succeed in accurately representing the 20% of the American population who is disabled by ensuring that at least 20% of their cast and creative team are disabled. Currently 95% of disabled roles are played by non-disabled actors.

I am so pleased to know that because of NDT's educational touring show, three of the schools we went to have now made permanent physical changes to their buildings to be in compliance with ADA requirements. It was an absolute joy and honor to have played a part in making such change happen, and to know that disabled children in these schools will have a better shot at access to the same opportunities as their non-disabled peers.

However, my commitment to change drives my decision to resign. Although I experience oppression and discrimination every day as a person who is autistic and legally blind, and experience the trauma of grieving the weekly death of a disabled person at the hands of their parent or caregiver, I also recognize the immense privileges I have as a straight white man. I've also been determined to use those privileges to pass focus to those without those same privileges. The privileges I have came into play in the creation of NDT and my role within it, and I think the next step I can take to make NDT a more equitable organization is to now vacate that space insisting to be replaced by a disabled BIPOC. I believe that a true rising tide lifts all boats. I believe that if ever the white supremacist, ableist, heteronormative, cis-gendered patriarchy is going to be dismantled in this country, it is going to require ALL historically oppressed communities working together and supporting each other, and providing each other the allyship the white supremacist, ableist, heteronormative, cis-gendered patriarchy does not give to any of us.

The oppression and discrimination experienced by the disability community goes unnoticed by much of society. Did you know that forcible sterilization of developmentally disabled people such as myself is still legal and practiced? Did you know that the minimum wage does not apply to disabled people? Employers are legally free to pay their disabled employees as little as they see fit. In recent years, there have been reports of an estimated 420,000 disabled individuals who have been paid an average of just $2.15 per hour, and of disabled people being paid mere cents per hour. Did you know that 85% of autistic college graduates are unemployed? Again, for the last decade 85% of autistic college graduates were unemployed. With my resignation, I join their ranks. Did you know that 33–50% of people killed by police are disabled? Did you know that at least once per week a disabled person is murdered by their parent or caregiver, simply for being disabled? Our society wishes that people with disabilities would just disappear, and media coverage is either silent or overwhelmingly supportive of their murderers. The theatre community is complicit in this erasure.

I am exhausted from seeing cripface plays at theatres across the country, even those I am in residence at. For example the world premiere of "The Luckiest," where non-disabled playwrights, non-disabled directors, and non-disabled actresses playing disabled characters (using power wheelchairs, mimicking the speech and movements of a disabled person), inform the audience that it is better to be dead than disabled and burdening their friends and loved ones, before committing suicide. I am exhausted from having these theatre companies look at me and tell me that they don't see the issue, after I explain the issue to them. I am exhausted from Theatre Communication Group's conferences on diversity and inclusion never being accessible with captions, image descriptions, or anything else making it so disabled folx can attend these diversity and inclusion conversations.

A true rising tide lifts all boats. Anything else is just a wave. We are all stronger together.

I have sought to build bridges between NDT/the disability community and other marginalized communities. There has never been an instance of me doing an interview or public speaking engagement when I have not redirected the lens to Black excellence, female leaders or other members of historically oppressed communities who are being trailblazing, phenomenal leaders in the field. I have insisted on wearing Black Lives Matter shirts when being interviewed about autism by major television outlets in 2017, even when the networks discouraged me from doing so. I insisted that it was inappropriate for discussions about casting a trans actor to play a trans character to be happening without trans people at the discussion table for NDT's shows. I hope that other historically oppressed communities will work to similarly include the disability community or at the very least disabled members within their own community.

As many of you know, in November of 2019 I submitted a letter of resignation, having come to the conclusion that the unification of all historically oppressed groups unto the dismantling of overarching systems of oppression might be more likely achieved if a disabled BIPOC individual had my position in NDT. My resignation was not accepted last year, but I am submitting it again this year with an unwavering insistence on my stepping down. NDT was already planning on initiating a nationwide search for a BIPOC managing director after COVID-19 related gathering restrictions ease enough for theatres to resume operations, and I think our commitment to diversity at every level in theatre will be best shown if I also make my position available for filling, with my insistence that it be filled by a BIPOC individual. It is my hope that under its new leadership, NDT will continue putting forward diversity statistics the same or better than during my tenure as Artistic Director, and it is my hope that having a disabled straight white man step down from leadership in a disability rights organization will lead to other oppressed communities becoming allies stepping up for the disability community. It is my hope that seeing a white artistic director step down from their position of leadership will cause other white leaders to consider whether that is a necessary move for them also, making space for their talk about diversifying leadership to become action.

With love, gratitude, and respect,
Mickey Rowe

12

Darkness cannot drive out darkness; only light can do that.
Hate cannot drive out hate; only love can do that.

—Martin Luther King Jr.

Y ou never know where life is going to take you next, and that's okay.
Being fearless in the pursuit of our goals requires finding new ways to
stay the course. Sometimes everything will fall into place just the way we
planned it, but oftentimes curveballs will be thrown at us along the way,
which will require from us everything from recalibrating our plans to putting it all on hold indefinitely. Although I had eventually managed to get cast
in *Curious Incident* and start my own industry-changing theatre company,
I'd also had an abusive marriage and the fear of casting an autistic person
getting in my way. I had still not been cast in another role since *Curious
Incident*. I'd have to come up with a new strategy to keep pursuing my goal
of showing the world that autistic people, like my son "A," can work at the
highest levels in their fields. I eventually secured a fellowship with a local
cultural arts funding organization, and the funding from that allowed me
to produce a one-man clowning show called *The Fool*. Apparently that was
quite the conversation-sparking title. People wondered both privately and
in news publications about whether I was making commentary on society's
perceptions of people with developmental disabilities. Was I subverting the
fact that in medieval times it was common for the jester to be a person with
a developmental disability? There's truth to all of that, but really my most

conscious reasoning for that choice was because it described how I had felt about myself my whole life. The fool.

I rented out a 1920s vaudeville theatre that had been graced by the likes of Ella Fitzgerald, Ray Charles, and Jimi Hendrix. A cozy cavern of exposed brick, vintage velvet, and aging hardwood floors. I filled the small stage with clowning and magic props such as clubs, balls, a ladder, flash paper, torches, and a variety of old, dusty, wool felt hats. I dazzled a full house composed of family friends, students, and Seattle theatre industry folk. I juggled everything from eggs to bowling balls for them and made an empty wool coat come to life and dance around the room with me. I made fire and roses burst out of thin air, and sometimes I needed some audience assistance to make magic happen. What happened next was recorded and is still viewable on YouTube today! At the halfway point in the show, I let the audience know I needed a volunteer, the voice of a boyfriend who did not want to be at the show called out from the very back of the hall, "Choose Helen!" and after the show . . . we met . . . with a hug.

A year later when Helen found out that I was now a single dad, she immediately volunteered that we should go on playdates together. I had long thought that Helen was the most beautiful woman in the world. Helen was a badass, green card–carrying Asian immigrant from Australia. Though she paid taxes, she couldn't vote due to not being a citizen, but she also couldn't leave due to the fact that she had two children and a custody schedule that would require her to live in the U.S. until her children had flown the coop. Even though we would text about meeting up for playdates together with our kids, I would be paralyzed with shyness and lack of confidence and never followed through with actually scheduling or attending said playdate. I would just vanish into thin air, my lack of confidence turning me into a pale, vanishing, ephemeral ghost. I was making a fool of myself.

One day I saw a photo of petite Helen at Seattle's Fishermen's Terminal, surrounded by gruff men with weathered faces and white beards. Behind her was a fifty-foot-long pirate ship. I couldn't believe my eyes. I commented on the photo immediately, and Helen replied that she was in fact the general manager of the pirate ship *Queen Anne's Revenge*. "I can get you and your boys tickets to ride the boat tomorrow if you would like," she messaged. A real-life pirate ship. Just like the one my grandpa had built but larger, and not made of shipping pallets. I couldn't resist.

"Yes!" I immediately replied.

"Great, I have the day off, but my boys and I will ride the ship too! So we can get to know you. A playdate," she swiftly inserted.

A small aside, dear readers: Remember back when I was trying to film my audition for *Curious Incident* on Broadway? That was Helen who volunteered to film my sides with me, but I shyly ignored her because of how beautiful she was.

The next day, I saw the back of a large white hat. As it turned, there she was. Helen's large white circular hat made it look as though she had walked straight off a runway. Or no, that she had just hopped off a moped she'd been zipping around on through Spain. Her eyes had a warm but unwavering fire behind them and a clarity that I had never seen before. I normally hated direct eye contact, but Helen's eyes were magnets, and I couldn't pull away.

Her Malaysian Australian skin was olive colored, and her long, wavy, dark hair reached all the way down to the waistband of her skirt. Her voice was surprisingly resonant and deep for her barely five-foot frame. A richness that only really comes from bone-deep confidence.

The kids and I boarded the pirate ship. She stayed on the dock and walked to the heavy rope at the front of the ship, looking at the captain whose name I only knew as Scurvy Dog, and untied the rope that was securing the front of the ship to the dock. "Bow line free!" she yelled while throwing the rope onto the ship. "Nothing's free in life, girl!" the captain barked back at her. I assume he was joking. By this time she was at the other end of the ship and repeating the process, yelling, "Stern line free!" while tossing the heavy rope on board. She then placed her hands on the ship, her feet still on the dock, firmly pushing the ship away from the dock as the captain drove, before leaping, vaulting herself aboard. "So where were we?" she said. Her smile was so free. *Helen of Joy*. The face that launched a thousand ships.

I left that playdate unsure whether it had been a date for our four kids, or her and me. Barely two hours went by before I texted her hoping to find out. "To thank you for the adventure you gave my kids I'd love to take you out for drinks sometime. Or on a picnic on the beach. You choose." An hour went by and she hadn't replied. ". . . Or we can take our kids on another playdate sometime instead and that would be great too," I quickly inserted.

"If for our first date we have a picnic on the beach, can we go out for drinks on our second date?" she confidently replied.

A few months later we were a verified Brady Bunch for the twenty-first century. A disabled man and an immigrant woman of color trying to raise their four white-passing boys. What a responsibility. But luckily I was doing it with the kindest and most intelligent person I knew. I was so proud that my second marriage would let my disabled son know that he can hold out for the person of his dreams. When I first got married, I had listened to all those voices that told me that being disabled, I should feel lucky just to get to date anyone at all. They said I would be lucky if anyone married me. But I, I am the luckiest man in the world. My soul mate and best friend wanted to marry me. I always thought the phrase "Where have you been all my life" was just that, a phrase, a corny pickup line, but with Helen the phrase extended beyond a question and into a true existential yearning of the soul.

In bed, Helen liked how playful I was. It is easy to be playful when you don't know what any of the social rules are.

Even with my glasses off I can tell when Helen pulls a face at me in reaction to something I said. Even with my glasses off I can see that Helen is the most beautiful woman on earth. Though she does sometimes eat sour gummy candies while talking with me in bed at night after I have taken out my contact lenses. This way she knows I won't *see* her eating the candies, and then she won't have to share them and there will be more for her.

I had never really felt like I'd had a family. But now I had one. It had snuck up on me. It surrounded me. As did all four of our "Brady Bunch" kids. I belonged.

After I met Helen, other things magically started to fall into alignment. Things so magical that you wouldn't even believe them if I wrote them here. Things involving pirate flags and starry nights. Once we went to eat at Seattle's oldest Chinese restaurant. At the end of the night the waiter brought out a small tray with four fortune cookies on it. I reached for the one closest to me, but Helen stopped me. "You make your own fate," she said while shuffling the cookies about. After they were all sufficiently shuffled, we each picked a fortune cookie. When we opened them both, they both had the exact same message on them: "Dance as if no one is watching." When we got married outside, a cargo ship passed by, slowly chugging through Puget Sound with the initials HMMR printed boldly in white across the side of the ship. Our combined initials. Helen and Mickey Marion-Rowe. Once while on a road trip we talked about owning a sailboat one day; we said we would put two flags on it, an Australian flag for Helen and a pirate flag for me, one next to the other. We continued driving to the next town down the coast, and what did we see out on the water when we stopped the car in Astoria, Oregon? A small twenty-seven-foot sailboat with two flags flying, an Australian flag on the port side, and a pirate flag on the starboard side. But these things feel almost too special to even write here, friend.

I guess all I needed was love. Everybody deserves to be loved. That is not a special need. That is a human need. Everybody deserves to be loved.

Weeks after meeting Helen, I got the opportunity to workshop a show with one of my idols. David Shiner was a longtime clown at Cirque du Soleil and directed many of the Cirque du Soleil shows. He was also a Tony Award–winning actor and Bill Irwin's longtime Broadway clown partner. The producer had put us in a three-bedroom Airbnb overlooking the city for the duration of the workshop. David always played an angry clown with a very short fuse. Late one night David and I were sitting in the shared living room after a long day of clowning. He looked over and said to me, "I am not really David Shiner." "What do you mean?" I questioned . . . wondering if I was just being punked after finally believing I was getting to work with one of my idols. David said, "We must treat everyone we meet as if they are God or the universe just pretending to be a person for a short lifetime. We must treat everyone that way. Every single person on the street has that spark inside them." I tried to repeat this all back to him to show my understanding, but the Cirque clown just stared at me. "Well . . . yeah . . . but that's all just dense academic philosophizing. The point is: Be kind to everyone. Always. That's it," said the clown.

I hadn't so much as received an audition in two years when one day my inbox pinged with an out-of-the-blue offer to play the role of Mozart in the Tony Award–winning play *Amadeus*. Since the role was being offered to me without even an audition, I was sure that Mozart had a walk-on role, a cameo character who just walked across the stage at some point in the play about this Amadeus guy. "Sure," I quickly replied to the email in the same dry tone I used in middle school with the girl who wanted to borrow my pencil. When I began to research, I of course realized the composer's full name was Wolfgang Amadeus Mozart. In a full-circle moment, I remembered that it was Wolfgang Amadeus Mozart who had written *The Magic Flute*, which was the opera that tiny Mickey on stilts had showed up to audition for so long ago.

This was the first show in *years* I had gotten to even audition for where the play was not about autism and autism was not the first word in my character's description. Representation matters, and it's really beneficial for the one in fifty-four kids who are diagnosed with autism, as well as society as a whole, to experience autistic actors in roles that would be typically cast with a nonautistic actor. But in an interesting twist, the Amadeus story line about the one-sided rivalry between Mozart and Salieri was first created by the Russian poet Alexander Pushkin, who was likely autistic himself. While he is considered by some to be the greatest Russian poet and the founder of modern Russian literature, he could not manage life skills and executive functioning. He could not understand the arbitrary social and societal rules for politeness, which led to him at one point being exiled from Russia. He felt so depressed about not being able to function socially and otherwise that he wanted to find someone, anyone, who was like him and write *that* story. The story that he needed to read. To make himself feel okay and acceptable. He found Mozart, who could not understand social rules, could not climb or understand the social hierarchy ladder, could not fit in the box, had no executive functioning, and died poor and broke, rejected by the court for not understanding *how* to fit into their box. Mozart himself may well have been autistic. All that autistic history is erased, and the story never reaches its fullest capacity when nonautistic actors are the norm. By casting an autistic person in the role, the story was heightened and enriched. I am so beyond honored that I got to bring this story to life onstage with this incredible and talented group of people.

I believe that acting is empathy. To be a great actor you have to have empathy. An actor's job is to know themselves incredibly well so that they can share all aspects of their humanity onstage. An actor needs to know what they are and just as importantly what they are not. When we practice empathy toward others, our job should also always be to begin by looking at ourselves. As hard as we work to see how our enemies are different from us, we must work equally hard to understand how we are like them. We must work to find what we can learn from and appreciate about our enemies' differences.

So, here is my technique for acting, or for you nonactors, my technique for empathy. When I play a character, I am not trying to "put on" something different from myself. I am trying to better understand myself. *What are the ways the character is similar to me, and what are the ways the character is different from me?* I can't answer these things if I don't really know myself. I am always going to be 5'5". I am always going to be white. I am always going to be autistic. There are things about me that will never change. Instead of pretending that these things about myself are not true, I instead try to accept them and understand them. I am honest with myself about who I really am. Only then can I look at my character: In what ways is this person, who may seem very different from me, actually very similar to me? I make a Venn diagram in my head with one circle that is Mickey and one circle that is this character who is very different from me. And then I try to move as many pieces from both of those circles into the overlapping section in the middle.

So, for instance, when I was playing Mozart in *Amadeus*—I know that I am very different from the wild blue-haired mastermind composer. But we also have so much in common. I know we both don't understand and thus have no regard for the social rule book. One mark for the middle of that Venn diagram. I know that in the play Mozart dies broke and starving. I know his wife Constanza handled all the bills, appointments, and managing of daily life. So both Mozart and myself lack executive functioning. Then I can better take note of the things that are actually different about me and Amadeus, and better understand where they come from. Only if I know myself well and have made this Venn diagram well can I truly understand what privileges I have. I can only be honest with myself about how someone is different from myself if I have truly dug deep and began by first looking at myself honestly. My strengths. And my weaknesses. We are all students of the human condition. May we each try to understand our enemies with as much heart, grace, and even love, as an actor tries to understand their character. That is what empathy is.

I threw myself into the role of Amadeus, who the Viennese court thought was so different from them, and boy, was it a ride.

The show was a stunning visual feast. The hats and costumes were luxurious and voluminous. The proscenium arch was opulent, and the raked stage featured Mozart's face, my face, painted on it larger than life. The wall towering over stage left was covered in a pop art–esque collection of Mozart portraits. The handmade wigs were numerous and wildly ostentatious! My favorite was bright blue, with a ponytail gathered by a bold pink bow.

The cast and crew immersed ourselves in a truncated rehearsal process, while the news whispered of a mysterious new virus in China. Everything abruptly accelerated over the course of the final two days of rehearsal before opening. COVID-19 tore through our country and Broadway closed the night before we opened. Our opening and closing nights were one and the same, and the local PBS station filmed our one single performance: New York's last professional pre-COVID performance before a live audience. It was such a history-making moment that the company sold out of the tickets that were released to digitally watch the recording.

When the reviewer at the *Wall Street Journal* saw this recording, they said, "Buy your ticket now, then come back and finish reading this review. . . . I don't know that I've ever seen a better small-screen version of a live stage performance. . . . Mickey Rowe giving a madly zany performance as Mozart. He reminded me at times of the young Jerry Lewis. . . . A triumphant demonstration . . . Artistically successful in every way."

The theatre was left empty. With the set still erect within it as chaos ensued in the outside world. All the lights turned out except for a single ghost light on a metal pole center stage.

All theatres have inside them a ghost light. A light that is always left on, shining bright, saying, "You are welcome," "You are seen," and most importantly "Don't fall off the edge of the stage, there." Even during the pandemic, these lights stayed on for the whole next year and more. Be that light for everyone around you. We need your light more than you know.

So, *Amadeus* had closed after one magical performance, the ghost light left on in the theatre. And I was back home at last. Home with Helen and my four monkeys. I had so been looking forward to the spring. The sun was shining even here in Seattle, and our four kids had been chomping at the bit to run wild in the sunshine after another rainy winter. My beautiful fiancée farewelled her twenties and turned thirty. And I was finally home after being away from my family off and on since January, first directing at the Tony Award–winning La Jolla Playhouse in California, then rehearsing and performing *Amadeus*. April was Autism Acceptance Month, and this year it was also the thirtieth anniversary of the passing of the Americans with Disabilities Act (ADA). April 2020 should have been one of the most peaceful and pleasant times of life for me: finally a fiancé to someone who deeply loved me, a father, and a theatre professional even though I was low vision and autistic.

But April 2020 saw the globe locked in the death grip of COVID-19. I saw a medical system buckling under the weight of skyrocketing cases of a terrifying new illness. Medical facilities were experiencing dire shortages of essential personal protective equipment like masks for their staff members, and therefore we heartbreakingly saw health care providers contracting and dying from the virus. Medical facilities were also experiencing dire shortages of the medical equipment they need to care for patients stricken by COVID-19, such as ventilators. In this situation where there was not enough necessary medical equipment, and with increasing numbers of nurses and doctors contracting the virus, difficult decisions had to be made as to how the limited available medical care was going to be rationed.

An increasing number of states and medical facilities created triage plans that recommend who should and should not be allocated lifesaving care. People with intellectual and developmental disabilities discovered with horror that they were at the bottom of the list. I was relieved to know that my nondisabled fiancée and three of our children were deemed worthy of lifesaving care. I was simultaneously bearing the crushing weight of finding myself at the bottom of my state's list, alongside my autistic four-year-old. In this age of COVID, if push came to shove, he might not be allowed to live long enough to achieve his dream of growing up to run his very own robot factory, simply due to his autism spectrum disorder diagnosis.

Decisions as to who was and was not worthy of medical care were being made in light of the CDC declaring that people with disabilities are at higher risk for experiencing severe illness due to COVID-19.[1] Decisions were also being made in light of the concept of Quality-Adjusted Life Years (also delightfully named QALYs), a concept and supposed equation discussed by the World Health Organization and others to determine how much less disabled people's lives are worth than their nondisabled friends', neighbors', and family members'. In its 2016 paper *Guidance for Managing Ethical Issues in Infectious Disease Outbreaks*, the World Health Organization states: "In general, the focus should be on the health-related benefits of allocation mechanisms, whether defined in terms of the total number of lives saved, the total number of life years saved, or the total number of quality-adjusted life years saved."[2]

Ari Ne'eman is a disability rights advocate, an expert on QALYs, a fellow autistic person, and a personal friend of mine. He described to the National Council on Disability what QALYs are and what they do, and it was published in its 2019 report delivered to the president. "The QALY works by weighting the lives of people with disabilities: If we were to assign autism a disability weight of 0.3, that [number] would mean that a year in the life of an autistic person would be worth 70 percent of a non-disabled person's life. Different disabilities would get a different number, if you assigned 0.5 to a mobility impairment, then a year in that person's life would equal 50 percent of a non-disabled life year."[3]

As a low-vision autistic man, father, and professional, I am here to say that my life provides just as much value to the world as yours does. My autism does not affect my respiratory health or immune system, but on this, the thirtieth anniversary of the Americans with Disabilities Act, Quality-Adjusted Life Years legally values me as less than a person just as Black Americans used to be valued as three-fifths of a person.

While most nondisabled scholars and medical professionals acknowledge the ethical shadiness of QALYs, they claim to have found a simple mathematical solution. As two such experts, Luis Prieto and José A Sacristán, state, "QALYs have been criticized on technical and ethical grounds. [. . .] Mathematically, the solution to these limitations happens through an alternative calculation of QALYs by means of operations with complex numbers rooted in the well-known Pythagorean theorem."[4]

Did you catch that? The Pythagorean theorem . . .

People love to infantilize me. Even though I am thirty-one, people treat me as though I am fourteen in most workplace settings. Now it all makes sense: they were using the Pythagorean theorem to calculate my disability-adjusted life years, much like one would calculate their fur-kid's "dog years." I see now.

People often talk about me using dog terminology. And I do love dogs. Dogs are often the only ones I have in any given room that accept me. I really do love dogs. Maybe dogs have aphasia. They can understand so much of what we say but can't speak. But when people try to lessen my humanity by using dog terminology to talk about me, I get . . . tired. I am extremely tired. As I am writing this, the top two stories in my social media feed are a story on the *Today* show about electric shocks being used to train "special needs" individuals to behave better[5] and an article in *People* magazine referring to a celebrity "re-homing" her autistic four-year-old. Stating that this celebrity couple was not the right fit for this child, so they are "re-homing" him into his hopefully "forever" home with a new family. I . . . I am tired. At least her son didn't fall into the statistic of the one disabled person who is killed by their caregiver every week. My friends. I'm tired.

Growing up I had been so optimistic! So bright eyed and eager. Now . . . I was getting depressed. I was tired. And I was done. Not because of my autism but because of how people had treated me because of my autism. But this is nothing spectacular. In 2014, a study in the United Kingdom found that out of 367 patients with Asperger disorder (known as autism now in the United States), 66 percent reported having suicidal thoughts and 35 percent reported suicide attempts or suicidal plans.[6] In fact, this is one of the reasons that the average life expectancy of autistic people is only thirty-six years old. I'm sure you can guess some of the other reasons the life expectancy of autistic people is so low. By this measure I still have five good years![7]

Disability gain refers to the good that comes from a person's disability: how it has positively affected their personality, worldview, creative problem solving, tenacity, and more. What theorem or mathematical equation has the CDC created to take into account disability gain? What theorem has the World Health Organization created to take into account the way my four children love me or the way I love them? How many Quality-Adjusted Life Year points does each kiss my children give me per day count for?

People are often surprised when they find out my beautiful, nondisabled fiancée is not my caregiver, though we do both help each other in many ways. I may be low vision, but I still know that I am married to the most beautiful woman on earth. How does the World Health Organization equate for the algebraic unknown that is my fiancée and our love? I may be autistic and low vision, but I contribute to society, however one could imagine they are godlike enough to quantify that.

And guess what, disability is the only minority group that is truly equal opportunity. Anyone can join our club at any time regardless of age, race, gender, or sexual identity. Everyone is just one accident away from having a disability. And should you be lucky enough to live long enough, you too will join our prestigious club one day.

Yes, triage is essential, especially in the age of COVID-19. But using a disability status alone to value someone's life as less worthy of ventilators is not only immoral and unethical, but illegal per the Americans with Disabilities Act, Section 504 of the Rehabilitation Act, and Section 1557 of the Affordable Care Act. And there are other options. As the National Council on Disability states, "The lives of people with disabilities are equally valuable to those without disabilities, and healthcare decisions based on devaluing the lives of people with disabilities are discriminatory. [. . .] There are alternatives to the use of QALYs [. . .] such as value frameworks that use patient preferences to determine the value of healthcare treatments. [. . .] Some stakeholders, but especially bioethicists and people with disabilities, have argued that QALYs are built on a faulty premise: that life with a disability is inherently worse than life without a disability."[8]

One example of this was recorded at St. David's Hospital in Texas as they refused COVID treatment to Michael Hickson because he was disabled.[9] As the doctor spoke, Michael's wife Melissa Hickson turned on her phone and began recording:

ST. DAVID'S DOCTOR: The issue is, will this help him improve his quality of life? Will this help him improve anything? [. . .] and the answer is no to all of those.

MELISSA HICKSON: What would make you say no to all of those?

DOCTOR: Cause right now, his quality of life—he doesn't have much of one.

MELISSA: What do you mean? Because he's paralyzed [. . .]?

DOCTOR: Correct.

MELISSA: Who gets to make that decision whether someone's quality of life, if they have a disability that their quality of life is not good?

DOCTOR: So it's not me, I don't make that decision. However it's will it affect his quality of life, will it improve his quality of life and the answer is no.

MELISSA: Why wouldn't it? Being able to live isn't improving the quality of life?

DOCTOR: [. . .] His quality of life is different from theirs. They were walking and talking people. And I don't mean to be frank or abrasive or anything, but at this point, we are going to do what we feel is best for him along with the state and this is what we decided.

Michael Hickson was a father of five.

I know, in your life, people tell you that the things that make you different are shameful. They aren't. I know that in your life society tells you that you should just fit in and make the things that are different about you disappear. Don't listen. Be you.

I do not think this doctor at St. David's is a villain or an evil person. I think he was ignorant and doing the best he could with what he knew. Everyone is always doing the best they can with the knowledge they have at the time. And we must allow people the opportunity to change! My mom was doing the best that she could with the skills and information she had at the time. And slowly over the years our relationship has improved! Both she and I have changed in many ways. When my ex-wife injured our child, she was coping with life as best as she could with the skills she had at the time. Her mental health was not her fault. And she has changed! She now sees a therapist and psychiatrist and works to be a very loving mother. Forgiveness is a gift that you give yourself. I also know that people grow. Even when I look at our politicians I try to understand and believe that the people who do the most harm to others are just . . . scared. They are just terrified. We should feel sorry for these people, for how fearful these people are. It does not make their actions at all okay, or at all acceptable, but let's still remember that if someone is not kind to you, they are probably not kind to themselves either. Being brave means being brave enough to do what is right even if it costs you, and even when nobody will notice. Being brave enough to fight for others and the environment even if you will not be alive to see the results of your work.

If you punish someone for making a mistake, that person will hide their wrongdoings, cover them up, make excuses for them, and defensively push the blame onto others to justify their mistakes. They will dig in their heels and are so unlikely to change. This leaves no one satisfied!

If you treat being wrong like a learning opportunity—because we have all been wrong before at different times in our lives—people's defensiveness falls away. They are more likely to admit their faults. They take responsibility. And they change.

In the UK, both the Care Quality Commission and the National Health Service sent warnings out to doctors after numerous people with developmental disabilities were having blanket do-not-resuscitate orders placed on them by their doctors. The memos explained that a developmental disability like autism does not automatically necessitate a do-not-resuscitate order, and that such decisions being made without input from the patients or their families is an unlawful breach of human rights. It is appalling to me that so many doctors, with their oath to do no harm, thought it was perfectly reasonable to decide to not help patients with developmental disabilities during the COVID pandemic. It reeks of assuming that people like me would not want to be resuscitated anyway, because who would want to live with autism? Society tells us better dead than disabled, right? Make disabled people and even the word "disability" disappear, right? It is one thing for society at large, that may not be well educated on disability or ethics and has no obligation to save anyone's life, to think that it's better to be dead than disabled. But it's especially sickening when medical professionals, who study for years to have the ability to save lives, also agree that it's better to be dead than disabled. This is when Shakespeare says, "When we are born, we cry that we have come to this stage of fools."

If you have any doubt what sort of stigma autistic people like me have to bushwhack through on a daily basis, consider this. Albert Watkins, the attorney defending the most high profile of the insurrectionists who invaded the Capitol building on January 6, 2021, has been blaming autism as the leading cause of the insurrection. Yes, as crazy as that sounds, you read correctly. To defend his clients he has publicly been saying, "A lot of these defendants—and I'm going to use this colloquial term, perhaps disrespectfully—but they're all f—ing short-bus people. These are people with brain damage, they're f—ing ret—ed, they're on the goddamn spectrum." This adds incredibly to the stigma faced by people on the autism spectrum every day. And I thought I had thick enough weeds to whack through already. It is worth adding that none of his clients actually are known to be autistic, but that doesn't even really matter. The saddest part is that no one really seemed to even care about Mr. Watkins's comments. But in the end, me being angry at this man doesn't hurt anyone but myself. And more and more I find that I just don't have the energy left to be angry. There is enough anger in the world. And with the box our world tries to fit disabled people into, why should we even be surprised by these comments? Can we really blame him?

On the other hand, can you imagine how advanced society would be right now if all through human history women were allowed to have jobs, Black people were not being put in menial positions, and disabled people were not either being killed at birth or put in institutions? Can you imagine where we would be as a society if everyone, with their diverse lived experiences and brain wirings, had been allowed to contribute to society? As Stacey Park Milbern said before her passing, "Ancestorship, like love, is expansive and breaks manmade boundaries cast upon it, like the nuclear family model or artificial nation state borders. My ancestors are disabled people who lived looking out of institution windows wanting so much more for themselves. It's because of them that I know that, in reflecting on what is a 'good' life, an opportunity to contribute is as important as receiving supports one needs."

I did want positive change. So, I went to protest. I tied my fabric face mask tightly around my face, boarded the bus in Seattle, eyed the sign at the front of the bus that read, "Essential Trips Only," and I headed into the city. It was dark and crowded. I didn't have a sign, nor a leaf blower or umbrella to repel tear gas. Just myself, my cloth face mask, and my hoodie for comfort. To this autistic person, protesting felt a lot like my old safe haven of being alone on a street where nobody knew me. It felt silent even though there were the sounds of chanting. I felt alone even though I was surrounded by people. It felt too dark and cool to be the middle of summer. It's like there was so much stimulation that it reached a tipping point where everything fell away. I was alone in the bubble of my brain. The protests were for an incredibly worthy and important cause: to condemn police brutality toward Black people and to assert that Black Lives Matter. Speakers at the protest reminded all gathered there that with a disproportionate 32 percent of people killed by police being Black, it is clear that Black lives do not matter to this country.[10] I was wholeheartedly grounded in agreement. I tried to hold these individuals in my thoughts while I protested, but my thoughts kept fluttering. How was I supposed to be acting? What was I supposed to be doing? Was I protesting just by standing among the crowd? My thoughts also fluttered as I secretly knew that my community was the most likely of any group to be arrested[11] or killed by a police officer with 33 to 50 percent of people killed in police interactions being disabled, though I couldn't say that out loud. I secretly marched for these invisible disabled folx too. I rode the bus home and then once off the bus shook the traces of 2-chlorobenzal-malononitrile powder from my hair. I hoped the night wind would carry it far away from me. Though I had done little more than walk, I had no energy left to think. To feel.

We live in a time where hatred, vilification, separation, and us-versus-them are held up above love and unity. Compassion and empathy can change the world. We all must learn from each other. There is something everyone can learn from you and you can learn something from everyone else and only together can we unite, bring hope to, be a light for, and heal this world. To condemn someone before you understand them only divides us more. Only makes that divide of misunderstanding greater.

Slow down. Listen. Your greatest enemy has something they can teach you, and you have something you can teach them too.

We must in all things work for understanding, not for a greater divide. Scarcity mindset leads to a lack of morality and greed. There is enough. You are enough. In every single interaction are we fighting for greater understanding or greater divide?

It is so easy to place the blame for all the world's problems on those you disagree with most. Instead we must all work for hope. For unity. And for healing. We *must* do this because no one ever thinks that they are the bad guy. Everyone always sees themselves as the hero who is in the right. Even those who commit the worst atrocities truly feel that they are acting on the side of good. At the least, we must fight for deep mutual understanding.

If we did this, maybe the government would care as much for our planet and the working class as it does for the stock markets and the megarich. We have the technology. The wealth is out there. The only question is do we have the morality.

Being brave means being brave enough to act with an open and vulnerable heart. Being brave means being brave enough to choose love over anger and fear. You can be the change. If your voice didn't hold any power, people wouldn't work so hard to make you feel so small.

Scientists all over the world have raced to develop a vaccine for COVID-19. However, a 2020 study found that at the time of writing this, only 50 percent of Americans plan to get a COVID-19 vaccination.[12] This falls far short of the 70 percent immunity that epidemiologists say society needs in order to truly and permanently break the pandemic. This isn't just isolated to America. "Vaccine hesitancy" made WHO's 2019 list of ten major global health threats. Most of those who aren't planning on getting the COVID vaccine have made this choice due to fears that it will cause autism. While there have been no credible scientific papers linking vaccines to autism, let's for a moment just imagine that vaccines did increase your chances of autism. We know that they don't, but let us imagine that they did. My life has not been a death sentence. Being connected to a ventilator while your lungs fill with fluid because of COVID-19 or any other preventable deadly disease *is* a death sentence. But my life has been incredible. My life has been wonderful.

And I would do it all again if I could.

13

If we are to achieve a richer culture, we must weave one in which each diverse human gift will find a fitting place.

—Margaret Mead

My clenching hand brings me back to remembering I am washed in that glaring spotlight, with the mammoth *Wicked* set pieces hanging down from above. The Gershwin's wooden industrial stage sturdy beneath my feet. I glance out at my spellbound audience filling each and every velvety seat of Broadway's biggest house. My chest is trembling. The set pieces hanging above my head immediately remind me of some of the lyrics sung by *Wicked*'s misunderstood green witch before her community wishes her melted with a bucket of ice-cold water: "I'm through accepting limits 'cause someone says they're so. Some things I cannot change but 'til I try, I'll never know!" I feel a bolt of power and resolve through my chest. I blame all the movie and theatre quotes in my head on the echolalia, the word describing how lots of autistic people would rather think in movie quotes than in their own words.

Having lost my train of thought for just a moment and needing to recenter, I glance back down at my notes on the lectern and also catch a glimpse of the wedding band Helen gave me glinting in the spotlight. *What has my life been?* My eyes work to hold the weight of a briny drop. Focus. Finish the speech. Squeeze hand once. Squeeze hand twice. Continue:

"And to those in the room on the spectrum," I loudly beg, making sure to take in the very sides of the room, and the back row of the expansive balcony, "what I ask of all of you today is this: Know yourself well. Know yourself well enough to understand that your differences are your strengths. Be brave. Jump in headfirst even when you aren't sure and be brave enough to advocate for yourself when you need something. Will you fail? Of course! Frequently! But will it be worth it? Yes. If I hadn't been brave and taken leaps that I was afraid to take, I would have never gotten to be onstage in *The Curious Incident of the Dog in the Night-Time*. I wouldn't get to be onstage here tonight, at the Gershwin Theatre on Broadway. So please be brave, ask for what you need, and trust that sometimes if you take a leap, the net will appear for you. Go be incredible, and more than anything, be you!"

One final thought rushes through my head, of Christopher's last unanswered line in *The Curious Incident*.

"Does this mean I can do anything?"

END

Thank you so much for taking the time to read this book. I hope you felt seen, understood, and silently heard. All I can do is share my story. Now you need to help keep this change going. Now it's time for you to tell your story. Now it's time for you to embrace your differences.

It is really important for me to hear as many of your stories as I possibly can! And to get to meet as many of my readers as I possibly can!

Share a photo of yourself with this book using the hashtag #FearlesslyDifferent for a chance to win a dinner with both me and my wife Helen for just you or a group of your friends. Multiple winners will be chosen! I want to meet as many of you as I can and hear your life story.

Or share how your differences are your strengths. I want to hear your story of dynamic empowerment using the hashtag #FearlesslyDifferent.

Thank you so much for getting to know me and taking the time to be an ally to both me and the disability community.

Most importantly, don't miss chapter 14 of the book. The longest chapter in this book, which begins immediately after this thank-you.

With deep gratitude and respect,
Mickey

14

Below is a list of the disabled people who were killed by their family members in the years 2014–2019 simply for being disabled. This list is not comprehensive and only includes those individuals whose deaths made news. The list below does not reflect the fact that up to 50 percent of people killed by police in the United States are disabled or that over half of disabled Black Americans can expect to be arrested by their mid- to late twenties. It only includes those people with disabilities who were killed by their families. For more information on any of these individuals, you are encouraged to visit www.disability-memorial.org.

2019 (102)

Zha-Nae Wilkerson, 9, January
Keith Theriot, 50, January
Tina Stimmell, 56, January
Heidi Winchester, 50, January
Willie Moore, 60, January
Sudesh Gupta, 67, January
George Rusnack, 73, January
Deborah Lynch, 62, January
Chet Scharnick, 84, January
Elvis Dry, 61, January
Anita Arias, 87, January

Sharon McManness, 75, January
Donna Featherstone, 78, January
Julie Kneifl, 72, January
Mia Edmundson, 9, February
Chun Li, 35, February
Theresa Bagwell, 58, February
Evelyn Scott, 77, February
Mary Fitzgerald, 85, February
Kiyoshi Suzukawa, 81, March
5-year-old girl, March
Kazuno Soeda, 6, March
Harish, 28, March
Santosh, 25, March
Ashlyn Ellis, 14, March
Ja'hir Gibbons, 2, March
Kashaiah P., 40, March
Janette Dunbavand, 81, March
Rebecca Fogel, 22, March
Vivek Kakadiya, 22, March
Sam Koets, 16, March
Kylee Willis, 4, March
Linnie Everett, 80, March
Tika Young, 37, March
Paula Meadows, 83, April
Jaden Webb, 8, April
Jorden Webb, 8, April
Sarah Dubois-Gilbeau, 5, April
Dhunalutchmee Naidoo, 69, April
Alexandra Jacobs, 77, April
Robbie Ballenger, 8, April
Andrew Freund Jr., 5, April
Duke Flores, 6, April
Gwendolyn Thombleson, 66, May
Mavis Long, 77, May
Esther Wavinya, 37, May
Steven May, 50, May
Sachio Uzue, 86, May
Eiichiro Kumazawa, 44, June
Betty Crews, 72, June

Alma Shaver, 80, June
Wilma Melchert, 85, June
91-year-old woman, June
Darlene Conger, 66, June
Shabhana, adult, June
Kushal, 2, July
Ashamati, 75, July
Syamala, adult, July
Mya Ase, 7, July
Ari Ase, 8, July
Kiyoko Otsuka, 96, July
John Savage, 3, July
Unknown woman, elder, July
L. A. C., 6, July
Marge, 83, July
Gail Camerota, 79, July
Sbusiso Mhlanga, elder, July
Malachi Lawson, 4, August
Cristina Pangalangan, 13, August
Patricia Whitney-Jones, 76, August
Victor Villa, 75, August
Adam Schneider, 39, August
Vanessa Mayfield, 31, August
14-year-old girl, August
Polly Bahadoor, 83, August
Dinah Durham, 65, September
Amzin Shaw, 63, September
Skylea Carmack, 10, September
Hector Pizarro, 16, September
"DH," newborn baby girl, September
Jakie Toole, 5, September
Joel Parks, 30, September
John Robinson, 47, September
G. B., 6, September
Conner Snyder, 8, September
Sandra Shaffer, 65, September
Mildred Costanza, 78, October
Jaime Feden, 33, October
Dorothy Davis, 77, October

Aiko Matsubara, 90, October
Jacqueline Juhlin, 50, October
Terri-Lynn Thompson, 54, October
Sefiah Hamid, 62, November
Shinobu Kishimoto, 95, November
Yoshio Kishimoto, 93, November
Takio Kishimoto, 70, November
Sharon Theleman, 51, November
Patricia Sander, 73, December
Sayoko Inada, 70, December
Mohd Amjad, 8, December
Harilal, 20, December
Masako Ikawa, 82, December

2018 (136)

Cristina Prodan, 27, January
Bhram Devi, 82, January
Sarah-Jane Gatt, 40, January
40-year-old woman, January
Sumiko Kobayashi, 84, January
Paola Manchisi, 31, January
Kakoli Das, 46, January
Lorene Hopkins-Pequignot, 69, January
Jeanette Brown, 74, January
Nancy Barclay, 83, January
Patricia Todd, 54, January
Adeline Hill, 66, January
Levi Illingayuk, 66, February
Tial Melvin, 22, February
Barbara Wilmes, 80, February
Akie Imai, 78, February
Andrea Bartlett, 38, February
3-year-old girl, February
Lerae Bush, 85, February
Akira Uwashitomi, 67, February
Jada Wright, 14, February
Daniel Stuart, 45, February

Belladonna Loke, 10, February
5-year-old girl, February
Cynthia Brunner, 74, February
Kenny Khan, 78, February
Liese Sparks, 57, February
Motomu Nomaguchi, 80, February
Yoshi Kinouchi, 86, February
Austin Steele, 18, March
Leo McWilliams, 84, March
Nathan Quezada, 21 months, March
Kaylina Anderson, 18, March
Aurelia Castillo, 14, March
Patricia Gottlieb, 83, March
Cody Nachtrab, 23, March
Susao Okuda, 76, March
Cheng Ting-hin, 6, March
Dinesh Sharma, 45, March
Samvith, 4, March
Douglas Fischer, 77, March
David Parton, 76, April
Nichol Widger, 20, April
Abraham Cardenas, 7, April
Amanda Zriny, 26, April
Susan Gibson, 75, April
Daniel Gibson, 17, April
Destiny Rollar, 22, April
Judith Howe, 73, April
Kathleen White-Gangruth, 61, April
Sharron Wood, 68, April
Betty Lyons, 85, April
Adeep Reddy, 9, April
Shashank Reddy, 10, April
Josephine Leong, 83, April
Frans Pitjeng, 48, April
Christopher Bosselman, 5, May
Aidan Talmage, 10, May
Tyler Talmage, 14, May
Kadyn Cockman, 8, May
Taye Miles, 13, May

Arye Miles, 10, May
Rylan Miles, 12, May
Shefali Samanta, 42, May
66-year-old man, May
Antoin Hawes Jr., 28, May
Pearlie Williams, 77, May
9-month-old baby, May
Bernadette Green, 88, May
Heaven Watkins, 11, May
Wilson Ross, 74, May
Mary Smith, 88, May
Philip White, 65, May
Joshua Alonzo, 21, May
Sumitra, 7, May
Denise Rosser, 38, May
Mae-Kim Lem, 76, June
Chloe Hobbs, 11, June
Sharon McCleary, 63, June
Bertha McGill, 68, June
Hayat, 65, June
An Ja, 76, June
Je'Hyrah Daniels, 4, June
Xuan, 9, June
Peggy Pettis, 64, June
Vanessa Comer, 21, July
Patricia Franks, 86, July
Jacob Edwards, 6, July
Dawn Liebig, 46, July
Barbara Lewis-Brown, 77, July
Laurel Bentley-Bearham, 91, July
Ernest Starry, 85, July
Helen Smith, 81, July
Emma Bingaman, 2, July
Stephanie Packman, 64, August
Sharmila Devi, 36, August
Mary White, 92, August
Ann DeLucia, 70, August
Muhammad Rabiul, 30, August

Ronald Blankenship, 64, August
Mason Jordan, 7, August
Bonnie Hanks, 52, August
Jalen Goldsborough, 13, September
Dante Mullinix, 2, September
Mary Terry, 79, September
Evelyn Bailey, 93, September
Stacy Hunsucker, 32, September
Logan Starling, 4, September
Ecie Gabrielsen, 79, September
Jonathan Schmoyer, 2, September
Sadhana, 9, October
Shobha Kulkarni, 75, October
Shuji Sanada, 49, October
You Su Kim, 74, October
"Miss He," 3, October
Irma Reese, 84, October
Linda Sweat, 77, October
Gina Riccò, 84, October
Kelly Barber, 57, October
Gabrielle Michaelis, 58, October
Ann Pomphret, 49, November
Emily Hampshire, 14, November
73-year-old woman, November
Cyra Harrison, 25, November
Patricia Way, 76, November
Kyoko Naito, 69, November
Hiroki Naito, 36, November
Michael Keene, 51, November
June Knight, 79, December
Rebecca Ballenger, 70, December
Yulia Nezhikhovskaya, 32, December
Frank Novak, 92, December
Sheila Small, 73, December
Delanie Manning, 68, December
Baby boy, 29 days, December
John Likeness, 54, December

2017 (173)

Victoria Cherry, 44, January
Mercedes Witterman, 69, January
Alex Santiago, 21, January
Perleen Bode, 67, January
Yoko Kubota, 37, January
Karen Allen, 74, January
Scott McCallum, 55, January
Barbara Martone, 81, January
Irene McLean, 96, January
Marilyn Miller, 83, January
Ms. Tsang, 63, January
Peter Abrahams, 97, January
Rebecca Benight, 73, January
Michael Guzman, 5, January
Jose Gomez, 30, January
Erin Leinweber, 58, January
Ellen McKenzie, 48, January
Samuel Murrell, 87, February
James Smith, 68, February
Tina Billingham, 54, February
Robert Jones, 61, February
Joseph Bishop, 18, February
Sanaa Cunningham, 7, February
Erwin Drake, 93, February
Matthew Tirado, 17, February
Fung Shuk-ying, 56, February
Walter Clark, 63, February
Jocelyne Lizotte, 60, February
Brandon Strauss, 21, February
Cameron Hoopingarner, 9, February
Avis Addison, 88, February
Moti Sahu, 43, February
Shoba Singh, 50, February
Prakash Singh, 56, February
Nicholas Dean, 31, March
Jeffrey Franklin, 16, March
Ruth Bain, 82, March

Jhalandia Butler, 28, March
Refilwe Monamodi, 54, March
Maria Stiles, 90, March
Kanchana, 28, March
Amber Perry, 6, March
Jaylynn Keith, 27, March
Troymaine Johnson, 33, March
Chiaki Kino, 36, March
Noah Campbell, 8, March
Pamela Kruspe, 61, March
Wilma Paletti, 75, March
Charles Singer, 48, April
Estelle Swanson, 66, April
Tyson Clark-Robertson, 24, April
Walter Brown Jr., 24, April
Helen Dansie, 67, April
Manubhai Bujad, 55, April
Laxmi Naidu, 76, April
Rekha Baloliya, adult, April
Kentae Williams, 10, April
Kari Whitley, 43, May
Rollis Bowman, 76, May
Davarion Davis, 12, May
Herlene Narosa, 22, May
Yoshiaki Tamekiyo, 76, May
Murray Upshaw, 40, May
Li Mouyi, 46, May
Gail Caulfield, 75, May
Sabrina Ray, 16, May
Kathy Smith, 59, May
Nancy Gleisinger, 76, May
Lovedeep Singh, 12, May
Lorraine Smith, 53, May
Brianna Gussert, 13, May
Shakira Hicks, 35, June
Lam Mei-kam, 76, June
Henry Johnson Jr., 57, June
Colton Johnson, 2, June
Sandra Nickells, elder, June

Shirley Ervin, 69, June
Johnnie Ervin, 67, June
Grant Heckman, 28, June
Edgar Carbajal, 26, June
Ariful Islam, unknown, June
Mahalakshmi, 28, June
Peggy Schroeder, 53, July
Leona Twiss, 95, July
Micah Gee, 3, July
Olivia Gee, 2, July
Omar Omran, 3, July
James Walker, 72, July
Virginia Villa, 73, July
Dadirai Mashonga, 40, July
Ozlem Karakoc, 34, July
Palak, 14, July
Pernell Robinson, 49, July
Naoko Kaup, 84, July
Jonathan Crabtree, 26, July
Olivia Kray, 19, July
Shannon Cooper, 40, July
Mathew Dunbar, 42, August
Savannah Leckie, 16, August
Courtney Turney, 33, August
5-year-old girl, August
Ursula Cabalzar, 68, August
Donita Elliott, 47, August
Ann Marie Boardman, 70, August
Leah Cohen, 66, August
Vivian Nelson, 94, August
Margaret Sims, 70, August
Hui Yee Tang, 27, August
Rookiya, 5 months, August
Shirley Williamson, 65, August
Howard Quick, 66, August
Marion Reynolds, 22, August
Aishika Sarkar, 7, August
Hideko Mizutani, 90, August
Dominique, 8, August

Kiara LaSalle, 17, September
Shirley Thompson, 73, September
Kaylie Lis-Lalande, 9, September
Kyoji Hattori, 88, September
Elizabeth Lackey, 85, September
Frank Lackey, 89, September
Sarthak, 7, September
Varad, 7, September
Chatiya Wongthong, 15, September
Valerie Wallach, 61, September
Ryanna Grywacheski, 18, September
Kayden McGuinness, 3, September
Beverly Nickerson, 74, September
Swarna Kapoor, 62, September
Jayashreeben Nathwani, 64, September
Vanessa Danielson, 36, September
Antonio Di Stasio, 4, September
Julia Whitmore, 27, September
Nicole Beilman, 27, October
Jane Sergeant, 67, October
Richard Dubuc, 62, October
Olivia Cart, 5, October
Jeya Pichamuthu, 46, October
(Ms.) Liu, 77, October
William Dubois, 91, October
Masako Kumada, 61, October
Dayvid Pakko, 6, October
Sherin Mathews, 3, October
Elba Monroig, 61, October
Mason Blum, 2, November
James Chewning, 79, November
63-year-old man, November
83-year-old woman, November
Carolyn Croucher, 70, November
Charity Depina, 22, November
Kayla Hensley, 18, November
Dylan Davis, 11, November
Wade Denton, 49, November
Marcia Neigebauer, 63, November

William Brownlee Sr., 62, November
Meghan Scully, 38, November
Ruby Wilson, 94, November
Mariah Woods, 3, December
Fabiola Cosme-Feliciano, 19, December
Ninon Hardie, 72, December
Kendall Chick, 4, December
Aubrey Dawson, 5, December
Luke Dawson, 9, December
Logan Christy, 20, December
Irene Strandt, 81, December
Bruce Clayton, 70, December
Malu Devi, 26, December
Jordan Rodriguez, 5, December
Michael Shearin, 25, December
Airi Kakimoto, 33, December
Johnny McFadden, 19, December
Suneel Kotele, 40, December
56-year-old man, December

2016 (172)

Sophia Mahaffey, 19 months, January
Harmony Carsey, 2, January
Dwight Ridley, 59, January
Irene Carter, 78, January
Holly Lozon, 57, January
Phillip Maynard, 71, January
Bertha Coombes, 83, January
Adilynn Moseman, 5, January
Samantha Kelly, 39, January
Eunice Phiri, 53, January
Ameri Martin, 10, January
Ezra Miller, 6, February
Daniel Joost, 18, February
Rebecca Cutler, 26, February
Holli Jeffcoat, 18, February
Ethan Okula, 10, February

Carolyn Taurino, 57, February
Jeffrey Rak, 58, February
Desmond Hudson Jr., 6 months, February
Deborah Harris, 22 months, February
James Hill, 33, February
Nancy Parker, 75, February
Priscilla Edwards, 78, February
Maddox Lawrence, 22 months, February
Henry Mokoshoni, 9, February
Jessica Cunningham, 15, February
Dawn Green, 69, March
Tamra Turpin, 36, March
11-year-old girl, March
Michael Furst, 24, March
Mirella Guth, 64, March
Ronald McCabe, 56, March
Roberta Rybinski, 51, March
Cynthia Busch, 24, March
Tony Myhand, 59, March
Mary Palley, 73, March
Kobe Shaw, 9 months, March
Bethannie Johnson, 3, March
Kazue Kawazura, 53, March
Kenneth Nix, 69, March
Luciana Torcello, 82, March
Cathy Evans, 65, April
Yusei Ikeda, 11, April
40-year-old man, April
Masano Yao, 79, April
Yutaka Nagao, 61, April
Emily Perrin, 4, April
Adrian Parmana, 16, April
Maria Branco, 78, April
Whitney Chilumpha, 23 months, April
Enelesi Nkhata, 21, April
Lynda Cestone, 56, April
Jack May, 89, April
Barbara Kavanaugh, 88, April
Inaya Ahmed, 14 months, April

Cecilia Madray, 76, April
Patricia Myers, 69, April
Laraine Rayner, 52, April
Melissa Couture, 38, April
Patricia Gordon, 63, April
Marie Stempinski, 72, April
16-year-old girl, May
Kayce McDermed, 16, May
Gertrud Sigman, 92, May
Leslie Denn, adult, May
Ava Cole, 8 months, May
Carolyn Hager, 78, May
Ruby Knox, 20, May
Henry Sochalski, 64, May
Venkatesh, 45, May
Jose Castillo-Cisneros, 3, May
Jazmine Walker, 6 months, May
Leonard Isequias, 52, May
Elsie Scully-Hicks, 18 months, May
37-year-old man, May
Amir Ross, 1, May
Kira Friedman, 2, June
Charlene Norris, 79, June
Billie Jo Quintier, 52, June
Noemi Villarreal, 45, June
Rietje Willms, 80, June
Jean Irwin, 83, June
Tammara Killam, 25, June
Margaret Sinclair, 85, June
Kathryn Ashe, 66, June
Mason Bryan, 4, June
Yuki Kawashima, 85, June
Cedric Page, 53, June
12-year-old boy, June
Ty Lee, 11, June
Shaelynn Lehano-Stone, 9, June
Jordan Burling, 18, June
Janelle Johnson, 5, July
William Lamar, 74, July

Rifat Mohammed, 3 months, July
Patricia Kearney, 56, July
Mirudula, 4, July
Jeffrey Kittredge II, 20, July
Kaushal Pawar, 14, July
Nadia Schaible, 91, July
Lydia Whitford, 18, July
Charlotte Hart, 19, July
Claire Hart, 50, July
Catherine Purcell, 68, July
Nancy Wright, 85, July
Margaret Mayer, 85, July
Angel Alicea-Estrada, 58, August
Theron Leonard, 24, August
Princeton Holloway, 3, August
Benjamin Mitchell, 3 weeks, August
Margaret Sanford, 73, August
Ernestine Tindall, 88, August
Gerald Sohn, 84, August
Barbara Getman, 39, August
Ronald Bettig, 56, August
Yonatan Aguilar, 11, August
Jean Constant, 87, August
Maddalena Pavesi, 83, August
Mindy Speck, 21, August
Austin Anderson, 19, August
Leslie Ramirez, 3, August
Margaret Shelton, 85, August
68-year-old woman, September
Henry Wilson, 70, September
Earl Coleman, 81, September
Stephanie McGeough, 54, September
Shobhana, 55, September
Erica Parsons, 13, September
Muhammad Wahab, 26, October
Sirajubai, 35, October
Masako Hirahara, 84, October
14-year-old girl, October
Mark Mellor, 31, October

9-year-old boy, October
Elisa Lutz, 11, October
Maria Lutz, 43, October
Martin Lutz, 10, October
Mohamad Abdullah, 11, October
Andreas Headland, 3, October
Vickie Balogh, 57, October
Natalie Finn, 16, October
Harold Nolan, 73, October
Grace Packer, 14, October
Patricia Swink, 66, November
Janice Frescura, 68, November
Robyn Frescura, 50, November
Andrea Spina, 22, November
Robert Wellburn, 72, November
Sharon Greenop, 46, November
Rebecka Pearce, 30, November
Isaac Ward, 2, November
Faith Wilson, 10 months, November
Tyler Caudill, 6, November
Sue Liner, 84, November
Henrietta Belcher, 69, November
Tevaun Williamson, 7, November
Devendra Prasad Misra, 27, November
Robert Libby, 94, November
John Owings, 65, November
Brayden Otto, 7, November
Carol Simon, 48, November
Chance Vanderpool, 4, November
Albert Weaver Sr., 84, November
Brayson Price, 5, November
Riba Dewilde, 51, November
Natasha Wild, 23, November
Aedyn Agminalis, 17 months, December
Danny Fernandez, 66, December
Phyllis Mansfield, 72, December
Kathryn Breen, 74, December
Sonia Riang, 45, December
Theresa Smothers, 87, December

2015 (159)

Hayden Dukes, 4, January
Owen Collins, 3, January
Lee Del Ratez, 40, January
Susan Winters, 48, January
Arthur Pelham, 66, January
Caryl Vanzo, 90, January
Barbara Beam, 82, January
Brenda Davidson, 72, January
Cyrus Buskirk, 8, January
Ena Lai Dung, 77, January
Iblah Pilo, 2, January
Kylee Forrest, 4, February
Liam Milne, 11, February
Angela Rios, 55, February
Aja Dasa, 16, February
Ellen Jackson, 66, February
Gertrudes Hollis, 74, February
Julieanne Cieslikowski, 16, February
Anthony Tomaselli, 85, March
Lori Decker, 45, March
Rachele Tyburski, 26, March
Wendy Blackstone, 49, March
Patricia Spencer, 76, March
Mark Green, 56, March
Izaltina King, 86, March
Ahziya Osceola, 3, March
8-year-old boy, March
21-year-old man, March
5-year-old boy, March
Seth Johnson, 7, March
Abdelkarim Elmezayen, 8, April
Elhassan Elmezayen, 13, April
Ashley Lovett, 27, April
Annie Ee, 26, April
Gary Blanton III, 5, April
(Boy) Lin, 8, April
20-year-old man, April

Aidan Fenton, 7, April
Umesh, 35, May
Brooke MacBeth, 28, May
Angel Goodwin, 10, May
Emily Janzen, 19, May
Malachi Golden, 4, May
Jody Hernandez, 31, May
Martin Duram, 46, May
George Philip Carter, 59, May
Louis Spires, 68, May
Fardeen Khan, 8, May
Thembisile Dlamini, 58, May
Dorothy Berry, 77, May
Thenmozhi, 18, May
Vasanthi, 16, May
Vasantha Kumar, 14, May
Leon Jayet-Cole, 5, May
Aiden Archer, 3, June
Abigail Cozad, 31, June
Gracie Buss, 4, June
David Matwiju, 64, June
Courtney Liltz, 55, June
Hiroko Ono, 83, June
Lorrie Rolen, 53, June
Kimberly Stern, 27, June
Jacklyn Nguyen, 2, June
Harold Ambrosius, 89, June
Nicholas Richett, 20, June
Debra Mae Shelton, 61, June
Cheryl Young, 55, June
Forgiveness Sibanda, 3, June
L'Naya White, 6 months, June
21-year-old man, June
Anne Schmidt, 73, July
Quincey Pollard, 17 months, July
Baby boy, 3 days, July
Lala Mardigan, 20, July
Jessie McCrimmon, 43, July
Meredith Jessie, 6, July

Andeng, adult, July
Maxwell Peterson, 16, July
Luc Baeyens, 48, July
Thandazile Mpunzi, 20, August
Jason Corbett, 39, August
Chaitanya Balpande, 13, August
Karen Passmore, 58, August
(Boy) Sulpizio, 7, August
Albert Vereen, 63, August
Melisha Mosier Ludwick, 38, August
Elaine Latshaw, 76, August
Joyce Taylor, 26, August
Jody Meyers, 20, August
Sharon Johnson, 65, August
Carolyn Hyatt, 43, August
Brian Darbyshire, 67, September
Meryl Parry, 80, September
La'Marion Jordan, 5, September
Sze-ming Chan, 10, September
Julie Collier, 55, September
Steven Reis, 55, September
Margaret Yamaguchi, 61, September
Jessica Hagan, 19, September
Rachel Murphy, 15, September
David Swallow, 49, September
Gurneer Chaddha, 3, September
Kathryn Burroughs, 35, September
Thelma Hayner, 84, September
John Pehota, 77, September
Justin Kirby, 26, September
Jhoel Noria, 12, September
Gulpreet Kumari, 12, October
John Craig, 53, October
Kenneth Mobley Jr., 30, October
Johanna Hove-Becker, 32, October
Andrea Lago Ordóñez, 12, October
Geraldine Chandler, 84, October
Emily Kaminski, 16, October
Mary Fields, 67, October

Janiya Thomas, 11, October
James Wilkerson, 67, October
Simone Mottram, 51, October
Maureen Boyce, 68, October
Corey Carpenter, 27, October
Ezekial Castro, 4, October
Shigeko Igarashi, 67, October
Alfonso Rafael Jr., 56, October
Vishal Gaikwad, 19, October
6-year-old girl, October
Sally Nelson, 63, November
Harold Grise, 68, November
Dustin Hicks, 14, November
Helious Griffith, 5, November
Johnny Richards, 63, November
(Ms.) Lin, 50, November
Gloria Reilly, 69, November
Hannah Warner, 16, November
Hakan Erdem, 12, November
Lia Cotroneo, 88, November
Zvonimir Petrovski, 67, November
Josephine Williamson, 83, November
Yoki Fujita, 81, November
David Fuhrman, 54, November
Adrian Jones, 7, November
Vincent Apilado, 79, November
Payal Sawant, 6, November
Malik Drummond, 2, December
Evelyn Harvey, 93, December
Antonio Tucci, 71, December
Bruce Rangitutia, 55, December
Violet Barker, 92, December
Carmina Brown, 27, December
Tyler Bryan, 3, December
Richard Brichacek, 63, December
Gregory Cortis, 68, December
Kazuko Saito, 43, December
Jermain Ngawhau, 2, December
Yasuko Uechi, 82, December

Donald Nieman, 89, December
Rita King, 81, December
Nada Bodholdt, 92, December
Mark Fulgham, 36, December
Paul Roddy, 55, December

2014 (105)

Michael Jones, 48, January
Saharah Weatherspoon, 23 months, January
Lena Smith, 45, January
Aidan Bossingham, 12, January
Bruce Simmons, 58, January
Susan Simonetti, 56, January
Frances Dresser, 86, January
Damien Veraghen, 9, January
Lucas Ruiz, 17 months, January
Ayahna Comb, 9, January
Jagtar Gill, 43, January
Vincent Phan, 24, January
Ramsay Scrivo, 32, January
Madoc O'Callaghan, 3, February
Bridget Charlebois, 22, February
Monique Johnson, 37, February
Lucas Braman, 1, February
Jean Chamberlain, 70, February
Blanche Cowan, 100, March
Billy Ray Young, 52, March
Harlan Haynes, 96, March
Alexa-Marie Quinn, 4, March
Anayah Williams, 1, March
June Lang, 75, March
James Sootheran, 59, March
Tyron Honeywood, 25, March
Liam Fee, 2, March
Hannah Hoag, 18 months, March
Jonathan Samuel, 13, March
Luke Schlemmer, 3, April

Robert Robinson, 16, April
Daniel Schlemmer, 6, April
Marvell Patterson, 11 months, April
Baby boy, 5 months, April
Otto Smith, 18, April
Caitlin Wentzel, 12, April
Olivia Clarence, 4, April
Ben Clarence, 3, April
Max Clarence, 3, April
Gabriel McFarland, 4 months, April
Kalib Smart, 17, April
Ramona Atkinson, 73, April
Jessica Watkins, 21, May
Magdalena Amunyoko, 26, May
Krystyna Waszynski, 86, May
Anja Dewees, 45, May
Heaven Woods, 5, May
Barbara Poucher, 86, May
Mary Driscoll, 94, May
Rebecca Cotten, 22, May
Shilpi Akter, adult, June
Samantha Marcus, 17, June
David Alan, 59, June
Sayane Kishimoto, 3, June
Kenyon Slacks, 3, June
On-Yu Choy, 15, June
Shirley Beck, 39, June
Theodore Meyer, 91, June
Marcia Clark, 83, July
Katharine Mihok, 8, July
Albert Franklin, 67, July
Jarrod Tutko Jr., 9, July
Linda Kelley, 18, August
Sophie Kostek, 88, August
Jacee Sanner, 10, August
Nancy Fitzmaurice, 12, August
Isaac Robitille, 13, August
4-year-old boy, August
Dane Hathman, 6, August

Joan Stack, 82, August
Mary Stack, 57, August
Francis Stack, 48, August
Raashanai Coley, 11, September
Kim Hunt, 41, September
Fletcher Hunt, 10, September
(Boy) Zhang, 7, September
Michaelina Simonetti, 93, September
Bessie Looney, 82, September
Noama Ware, 78, October
Joann Canfield, 72, October
Esihle Mosoeu, 2, October
Betty Rowland, 86, October
Patrick, 17, November
Jean Adams, 77, November
London McCabe, 6, November
Tyrael McFall, 2, November
21-year-old man, November
Maria Fuentes, adult, November
Jenhyla Simms, 6, November
Agnes Caviston, 92, November
Daryne Gailey, 29, November
Camaron Larson, 11, November
Brielle Gage, 3, November
Samauri Page, 14, November
Georgianne Woolum, 90, December
Pendo Nundi, 4, December
Elizabeth Siwicki, 89, December
Yana Voronova, 7, December
30-year-old man, December
Alex Robinson, 9, December
Rosemary Vincent, 58, December
William Collins, 92, December
Kendrea Johnson, 6, December
Hope Ruller, 93, December
Katherine Lavoie, 49, December

notes

CHAPTER 1

1. https://www.marketwatch.com/story/most-college-grads-with-autism-cant-find-jobs-this-group-is-fixing-that-2017-04-10-5881421.

CHAPTER 2

1. https://pediatrics.aappublications.org/content/142/3/e20180134.
2. https://www.apa.org/monitor/2011/02/postpartum.
3. https://www.huffpost.com/entry/nicu-moms-depression-help_n_5acf7e7ee4b0edca2cb74958.
4. https://rudermanfoundation.org/the-ruderman-white-paper-media-coverage-of-the-murder-of-people-with-disabilities-by-their-caregivers/.
5. https://www.huffpost.com/entry/murder-victims-disabilities-mercy-killings_n_58bd5abfe4b05cf0f401b603.
6. https://abc7chicago.com/news/abc7-exclusive-alexs-story/439605/.

CHAPTER 5

1. https://www.creativegroupinc.com/2017/10/17/the-real-cost-of-employee-turnover-and-how-to-reduce-it/.
2. https://www.forbes.com/sites/sarahkim/2019/10/24/sub-minimum-wages-disability/#18a15aeac22b.
3. https://www.mi-reporter.com/news/working-without-a-net-playing-with-fire/.

4. https://www.seattletimes.com/seattle-news/judge-rejects-seattle-center-rules-on -buskers/.

5. https://rudermanfoundation.org/wp-content/uploads/2017/08/MediaStudy-Police Disability_final-final.pdf.

6. https://www.ncbi.nlm.nih.gov/pmc/articles/PMC5678390/.

7. https://www.census.gov/newsroom/releases/archives/miscellaneous/cb12-134 .html#:~:text=JULY%2025%2C%202012-,Nearly%201%20in%205%20People%20 Have%20a,the%20U.S.%2C%20Census%20Bureau%20Reports.

CHAPTER 7

1. https://www.indiewire.com/2017/09/actors-oscar-nominations-disabilities-afflic tions-1201879957/.

2. https://groundswell.org/oscar-winners-often-play-disabled-characters-so-why -dont-we-see-disabled-actors/.

3. https://www.msnbc.com/opinion/oscar-nominee-plans-shatter-film-world-s-crip pling-ableism-n1265139?fbclid=IwAR0PkLt9PH8y2Voa8JasKEN_jJWjU9N06SQV b57uiHt_xT0WJ6_c-RqrSVg.

4. http://www.rudermanfoundation.org/wp-content/uploads/2016/07/TV-White -Paper_7-1-003.pdf.

5. https://www.healthline.com/health-news/the-debate-over-terminating-down-syn drome-pregnancies#1.

6. http://www.markhaddon.com/blog/aspergers-autism.

CHAPTER 10

1. https://www.salon.com/2017/05/15/mickey-rowe-the-curious-incident-of-the -dog-at-night-time-autistic/.

CHAPTER 11

1. https://www.wnycstudios.org/podcasts/radiolab/articles/g-unfit.

2. https://www.wnycstudios.org/podcasts/radiolab/articles/g-unfit.

CHAPTER 12

1. https://www.cdc.gov/coronavirus/2019-ncov/need-extra-precautions/people -with-disabilities.html.

2. https://apps.who.int/iris/bitstream/handle/10665/250580/9789241549837-eng
.pdf;jsessionid=95EFEED2E6F367F8FE9FBB9BDBA56280?sequence=1.

3. https://ncd.gov/sites/default/files/NCD_Quality_Adjusted_Life_Report_508
.pdf.

4. https://www.ncbi.nlm.nih.gov/pmc/articles/PMC317370/.

5. https://twitter.com/TODAYshow/status/1387393100612579333.

6. https://www.thelancet.com/pdfs/journals/lanpsy/PIIS2215-0366(17)30162-1
.pdf.

7. https://ajph.aphapublications.org/doi/abs/10.2105/AJPH.2017.303696.

8. https://ncd.gov/sites/default/files/NCD_Quality_Adjusted_Life_Report_508
.pdf.

9. https://www.npr.org/2020/07/31/896882268/one-mans-covid-19-death-raises
-the-worst-fears-of-many-people-with-disabilities.

10. https://www.ncbi.nlm.nih.gov/pmc/articles/PMC6080222/.

11. https://ajph.aphapublications.org/doi/10.2105/AJPH.2017.304095?fbclid=Iw
AR0qqA_MjUOvw4juOs6PpHLEEiTZcsvdn6u6iVGIrY8wOYu1gWhdot6Wt3w&.

12. https://www.theguardian.com/world/2020/may/27/americans-covid-19-vac
cine-poll.

about the author

Mickey Rowe (he/him) has had a prolific and varied career as an actor, director, consultant, and public speaker; he is now highly sought after both nationally and internationally. He was the first autistic actor to play Christopher Boone, the lead role in the Tony Award–winning play *The Curious Incident of the Dog in the Night-Time*. He has also appeared as the title role in the Tony Award–winning play *Amadeus* and more. Mickey has been featured in the *New York Times*, *New York Times Magazine*, PBS, *Vogue*, *Playbill*, NPR, CNN, *Wall Street Journal*, HuffPost, and *Forbes* and has keynoted at organizations including the Lincoln Center for the Performing Arts, the Kennedy Center, Yale University, Columbia University, Disability Rights Washington, the Gershwin Theatre on Broadway, the DAC of the South Korean government, and more. Mickey was the founding artistic director of National Disability Theatre, which works in partnership with Tony Award–winning companies such as La Jolla Playhouse in San Diego, California, and the Goodman Theatre in Chicago.